NOBLE

NOTES

On Famous Folks

NOBLE

NOTES

On Famous Folks

Richard Edward Noble

First Edition

ISBN 978-0-9798085-5-5

Published in the United States of America
by
Noble Publishing, 889 C.C. Land Road, Eastpoint, Fl. 32328

Interior layout and design by
Carol Noble

Contents

Interesting Characters *115*

Writers and Poets   157

A note from the author

Noble Notes on Famous Folks is, first of all, a book of historical essays. This is to say that they contain the opinions, insights, and interpretations of the author along with historical facts, quotes and situations. This is not a history book. It is a book about history.

This is my first volume of *Noble Notes*. It is meant to be an introduction. My goal is to provide the reader with information, some new ideas and a possible stimulus to learn more on his or her own.

These are notes that I have accumulated over the years. All these notes were originally written for my own edification and to assist my memory. You might look at this work as my homeschooled college diary or study notes. I'm a student, not a professor.

I've included in this volume a variety of ancient and modern characters ranging from Constantine to Bill Clinton. Some are treated humorously, some satirically and some seriously.

Other books by
Richard Edward Noble

HOBO-ING AMERICA
A workingman's tour of the USA

A SUMMER WITH CHARLIE
A story about the last days of a young sailor

HONOR THY FATHER AND THY MOTHER
A tragic novel

A LITTLE SOMETHING
Poetry and prose

THE EASTPOINTER
A collection from award winning newspaper
column

Philosophers

And

Scientists

Abelard (1079-1143)

Wow! The story of Heloise and Abelard is one for the romantic novelist. Abelard and Heloise are adult material that dwarfs the story of Romeo and Juliet to a cutesy type children's story.

Abelard is a famous philosopher and teacher. He was born in 1079 and died in 1143. He was a cleric and eventually became the Canon of Notre Dame. He was hired by a dude named Fulbert to teach his niece, Heloise, philosophy. Heloise was both pretty and smart. Though Abelard was concerned mostly with "universals" in his philosophy, he was very much concerned with Heloise and her various "particulars" in his everyday life. She readily took to philosophy ... and Abelard. It was only a matter of time before Abelard and Heloise were heavy-breathing in just about every unoccupied room in the castle.

Soon their sex-ploits were common talk all over Paris. Finally Uncle Fulbert became embarrassed and gave Abelard the boot from the castle. But Abelard was still very much hot to trot. He tried to talk a maid at the Fulbert mansion into sneaking Heloise over to the rectory for a little romp behind the sacristy. But the poor brown skinned, shapely maid was having quite a time of it herself. She said that she would only be willing to produce Heloise for a little heaven if Abelard would park his truck in her garage for a little hell on a weekend or two.

Abelard felt that such a suggestion was "universally" unacceptable. I guess he was too "particular."

In any case, Abelard dismissed the poor maid. She in turn went to Uncle Fulbert and told him all about Abelard's proposition. Uncle Fulbert was, to say the least, totally incensed. He decided to nip this little romantic adventure in the bud. He bribed a servant of Abelard to sneak into Abelard's bedroom while Abelard was sleeping and cut his "universals" off with a razor. Which he did!

After that, Abelard's life was religiously correct if not personally "upright." Abelard then went to an abbey and Heloise to a nunnery. From these outposts they communicated their passions to one another in a series of letters over the years until they died and were buried in a grave next to one another.

My God, what a story!

What is interesting to me is that most of my philosophy books give very slight mention to this story. Frederick Copleston S.J., for example, has this to say, "As a result of the episode with Heloise, Abelard had to withdraw to the Abbey at St. Denis."

That's it.

In the next paragraph, Copleston S.J. goes on to say, "Abelard was a man of combative disposition, and unsparing of his adversaries. He ridiculed his masters in philosophy and theology; he was difficult to get along with; and was unable to live in peace with the other monks."

Well, golly gee S.J., do you think that his irritable disposition might have something to do with the fact that he just had his you-know-whats cut off? No big thing to you, I suppose, S.J., but I could imagine myself being a little "out of sorts" for a week or two if I were in old Abelard's shoes. This "episode" would be a little difficult for me to generalize, even if I was a philosopher. But, I understand that this "particular" opinion of mine might not be "universally" acceptable.

Archimedes (287-212 BC)

Eureka! Eureka! (I have found it! I have found it!).
According to history and legend, this is what Archimedes went
running around the town of Syracuse screaming, one day. On
top of that he was supposedly naked as a jaybird. He had been
sitting in a public bath when he suddenly realized the
phenomenon that we call today "specific gravity."

It seems that his buddy, actually a relative of some sort,
King Hiero (Hieron) was having a problem with his jewelers.
Hiero had the suspicion that his gold crowns and other golden
paraphernalia were being "cut." They were spiking his golden
crowns and jewelry with silver or, even worse, lead instead of
100% genuine gold. The problem was in verifying his
suspicions.

Archimedes noticed that when he flopped into the tub at the
public bath, water came spilling over the sides. This led him to
experiment and, sure enough, he found that different metals
displaced different amounts of water. His dunking
experiments, comparing gold, silver and the King's crowns,
confirmed the King's suspicions. You can bet that there were a
number of Syracusean jewelers who suddenly found their own
bodies displacing less water than they had a week ago after
that knowledge became available.

Other tales about Archimedes are even more spectacular. He
supposedly defended the town of Syracuse for three years
against an armada of Roman ships and soldiers led by a Roman
general named Marcellus. He did it all with his scientific
genius. He invented new and unimaginable weapons of war. It
is alleged that he invented catapults that could throw a stone
weighing a quarter of a ton. He developed "burning mirrors,"
huge, shinny, reflective, metal shields, which he used to re-
direct the sun's rays to set the Roman ships in the harbor
ablaze. He then mined the harbor via a system of pulleys he
had somehow connected to a series of nets and grappling
hooks. These contraptions actually lifted the enemy's ships
from the bay and tipped them upside down or smashed them
against the rocks lining the shore. In the end, the Romans
finally sneaked into the city by land while the whole town was
involved in a drunken celebration. The seventy-four year old

Archimedes was involved in scratching out a geometric problem in the dirt when a Roman soldier ran him through.

According to legend Archimedes asked the soldier to please delay his sword until he had finished his problem. The soldier obviously did not share Archimedes interests in geometry.

Archimedes was a student of a guy named Canon who was in turn a student of the great Euclid. Euclidean Geometry is what saved Bertrand Russell from suicide. I had a similar experience, though it wasn't actually Euclidean Geometry that saved me from committing suicide. It was discovering sex that had the same rejuvenating effect upon me. But I consider the learning experience much the same for both me and Bertrand.

Archimedes gave us that famous mathematical symbol known as "pi." You remember - the area of a circle equals the radius squared times pi. That's the famous number 3.14. When you asked your high school, math teacher where the heck such a number came from, he said; "Just follow the formula and don't be wasting your peanut brain on such foolish questions. What the heck do you care where it came from as long as it works? Who do you think you are anyway, Albert Einstein for God's sake?"

He could have simply said that Archimedes made it up. That would have done it for me.

Aristotle (384-322 BC)

Aristotle was even richer than Plato. He came from money, married money, and was given money. He was loaded. This guy had more money than George Soros, and the Donald put together.

He liked books, read constantly and had one of the largest libraries of the day. He is credited with the publication of over a thousand volumes himself. He wrote something on everything. He was the Isaac Asimov of the neighborhood. The only problem is that just about everything that he wrote about, or supervised, on whatever subject, was wrong. Socrates is called the Father of Philosophy and Aristotle is called the Father of Science. You can read Socrates and learn about philosophy, but don't read Aristotle expecting to learn science.

Aristotle studied under Plato for either eight years or twenty-eight years, depending on who you read. Everybody seems to agree that Aristotle had a period of sowing wild oats before he settled down; they disagree on how long it lasted. After Plato died Aristotle expected to become Dean of Plato's Academy. It didn't happen. He wasn't a "local-yokel." So Aristotle split.

King Hermeias invited him to come and help govern his little province in Asia Minor. Aristotle did somewhat better than Plato in his attempt at government. Like Plato he got bounced, but Hermeias didn't try to kill him, nor did he sell him off into slavery as happened to Plato. Hermeias told Aristotle to move on, but he must have liked him, because he paid him to take his adopted daughter Pythias along with him. And he paid him well, too! Then, of course, we have no photos of Pythias either.

Aristotle was then offered a job by Philip of Macedonia, to teach his young, epileptic, homosexual, alcoholic, uncontrollable, belligerent nitwit of a son, later known as Alexander the (not so) Great. It didn't really work out. Teaching Alexander the idiot how to think was about as easy as teaching Helen Keller how to shoot pool. But, nevertheless, Philip ended up donating about $4,000,000 to Aristotle's cause. Aristotle must have had something or Philip was drunk once again when he signed the check. Aristotle then went back to Athens and opened his own Academy, the Lyceum. The school obviously attracted a lot of other little rich boys, and did well, but his association with Philip and Alexander would come back to haunt him. Needless to say Alexander and his "Paw-paw" were not well loved.

After his daddy's death Alexander kept conquering everybody. He liked hanging and crucifying people too. He hung Aristotle's nephew, Callisthenes, because he refused to recognize Alexander as a god. In any case, Alexander got into a drunken brawl one night and was killed. This was great for the world at large but not so wonderful for Aristotle. He had always defended Philip and little dysfunctional Alex ($4,000,000 buys a lot of good will). So when the people of Athens revolted, they reasonably decided to kill Aristotle.

Aristotle wisely decided to leave town. He didn't want to let the citizens of Athens "sin" against philosophy once again as they had with Socrates. It is claimed that he made a cup of his own Hemlock and killed himself anyway.

Before he died, he freed all of his slaves. Since he was a confirmed elitist, aristocrat and defender of the supremacy of "some" over the "many," I wonder why?

Aristotle vs. Galileo

Aristotle first observed that a body at rest tends to remain at rest and that it will not move unless acted upon by some external force. For example, a rock will remain on the ground unless somebody picks it up and throws it; or a bullet will remain in a gun, an arrow in a quiver, or a canon ball in a canon. Everybody seemed to like this type of thinking until Galileo came along.

Galileo, being an astronomer, concluded from his observations that a body in motion tends to remain in motion and will not be stopped or diverted from its course unless some sort of external force was brought into play. Scientists now claim that Galileo was correct and Aristotle was wrong.

In observing the planets and stars out in space Galileo does seem correct, but in observing the situation here on earth Aristotle seems to be doing fine.

The planets in space are in constant motion. But the question persists, how did they originally get moving? If you say that they are in motion and have always been in motion and that their motion is the product of mutually compensating, perpetually infinite initiatives, you are an atheist, or a pantheist or at least stating the divinity or eternity of the universe. I dare say you would agree with Galileo's observations and the notion that a body in motion tends to remain in motion and will forever do so.

If you say that the universe was initiated by a Big Bang, then you still must explain where the energy from the Big Bang originated. But the very fact that you postulate a Big Bang presupposes that you are really an Aristotelian. You are suggesting that bodies in motion need a start or an external force in order to get them into motion. You therefore must believe as your basic tenet that a body at rest tends to remain at rest and will only be put into motion by some sort of external force acting upon it. So then if Aristotle and Galileo are truly in opposition, your Big Bang stance suggests that you believe Aristotle and not Galileo.

Isaac Newton suggested that there was a force acting upon all bodies in the universe called gravity. He further stated that this force could be calculated, and he did so. But when asked

19

how everything got moving in the first place, he suggested that everything was first tossed into movement via the hand of God. God started motion by tossing the stars and the planets out into space, then instituted gravity and whatever other forces of nature to keep everything "floating."

To the followers of Newton, the world will end whenever God decides to remove his force or his hand in the matter.

To the proponents of the Big Bang, the universe will end when the energy expended in the Big Bang expires.

But, if Galileo speaks the truth, and "a body in motion tends to remain in motion" is the first principle of the universe, then there was no Big Bang and there is no need for a God, and just like "a country boy" the universe will survive.

Avicenna (980-1037)

Avicenna (Ibn Sina ... Abu Mi al Husayn ibn Abd-Allah ibn Sina) was born in Bokhara, Persia (Iran) in 980 A.D. He is most famous in the field of medicine. In fact his book, *al-Shifa* (Book of Healing) is the largest encyclopedia of knowledge ever written, and was the main medical source book for over four hundred years.

In physics he is the father of the notion of "momentum." By age ten he had mastered the "religious sciences" (whatever they are); by sixteen he was a well known physician; and by eighteen had mastered Aristotle, thanks to the commentary of al-Farabi.

Prior to reading al-Farabi, he had read Aristotle's *Metaphysics* over forty times and couldn't understand it. (So, how smart is he? I had to read Aristotle's *Metaphysics* only once to realize that I couldn't understand it.)

Avicenna was a mystic. A mystic is, in my opinion, a person who begins with the "fact" of God and then tries to prove the universe and all of reality a fiction.

In philosophy Avicenna is most famous for his concern with "quiddity" (essence) and distinguishing between it and existence, and also his arguments distinguishing between necessary and possible beings. An unnecessary existent (us and everything else that is) can exist or not exist, says Avicenna.

Is this true? The fact or truth is, we don't know. The theist says, in dealing with human existents for example, that when we die our body dies, but our soul (the electricity or force of consciousness and life) goes on.

The atheist says that our bodies are turned to dust and the force of consciousness of life vanishes. So one denies the immortality of the body and the other denies the immortality of the life force that distinguishes a dead body from a living entity. But the body turns to dust, it doesn't cease to exist. So then what happens to the soul - the animating life force?

No one knows. Is there such a thing?

We know there is. It is there when something is alive, and gone when something is dead.

Can anything that is existing at one point ever be non-existent? As Einstein once asked, "Did God have a choice in his own existence?"

We have a scientific law today that we call the conservation of matter and energy. Both Energy and matter cannot be created nor destroyed. God, according to Avicenna, is the only necessary being. But one of the qualities of the necessary being is that it can not, not be ... it must exist. But the law of conservation of matter says that this is true of all existing things. So then, do we conclude that God is all that is or exists, and that what is, is and has always been and will forever be?

Avicenna like all religious mystics establishes his philosophy on a weak foundation. He establishes as true, an unfounded assumption (God) and then attempts to coordinate reality to it.

Question: if every known and observable thing in the universe has a cause, why would anyone assume that the source of all would be un-caused? The only conclusion that can be reasonably drawn from the fact that every known thing has a cause is that all things yet unknown must have a cause also.

Applying this to a definition of God, we would not conclude that God is uncaused but that He must be an infinity of causes. If all known things are particular and variant, then God could not be one and whole but multiple and divisible.

Avicenna first believed in God and then the Koran (the revealed word of God). His goal was to establish God as true; revelation, as the Word of God; and all else subject to the knowledge of the two.

Francis Bacon   (1561-1626)

"If one must study logic, let him begin with this book."

This is the advice of Will Durant in his *The Story of Philosophy* with regards to the work of Francis Bacon entitled *The New Organon.*

Well, I have always been a person concerned with the art of correct and reasonable thinking. Even the word "logic" has always appealed to me. I decided to send for the book. But first, who is this Francis Bacon anyway?

Frank goes all the way back to the fifteen hundreds. He was around during the time of Queen Elizabeth, and Queen, I mean, King James I. Frank was from a very prominent family. His father and some uncles were big shots in the government, and his mother was an educator. But for some unexplained reason little Frannie gets left out of the will and ends up going to law school and becoming Attorney General and Lord Chancellor all on his own. How he found the money to do all of this isn't really explained, but it seems that Frannie had his ways.

He had a rich buddy named Essex who really, really liked him. Essex gave Frannie a home and a pile of acreage, and a monthly check just because he was cute, it seems. In any case, Frannie was so grateful for all of this that when the lord Essex got into a little trouble with the Queen, Frank, the now great orator and barrister, ran to his good buddy's aid.

By the time he finished speaking, without being asked, mind you, his good buddy and lifetime benefactor, who was instore for a slap on the wrist from the Queen, got his head put in a bucket. Frank wrote a lengthy explanation of why he spoke so about his good friend - which also sold out at the newsstands.

His next stepping stone to success came with his defense of King James' attitude towards people accused of a crime, volunteering information. King James felt that an hour or two on the rack or a couple of twists on the thumbscrews was within the realm of reasonable friendly persuasion. Frank agreed with the King and they became even better friends. And their friendship had nothing at all to do with the fact that they were both inclined to wear pink panties under their blue boxer shorts.

Unfortunately, Frank loses his fame and fortune when he gets caught taking bribes. Frank defends himself by saying that he wasn't doing anything that everybody else wasn't doing. Frank tops off this glowing career of logical reasonable thinking by going out horseback riding in a blizzard one afternoon. While out riding Frank gets the notion to kill a chicken and stuff it with snow to see how long a chicken stuffed with snow would stay dead, I presume. Well, while watching the chicken to see just how long a chicken stuffed with snow will stay dead, Frank catches cold and dies. The scientific question here is who stayed dead longer - Frank or the snow-stuffed chicken?

And Will Durant tells me that if I want to learn the art of logical, reasonable thinking, I should read Francis Bacon. I don't think so!

Tycho Brahe   (1546-1601)

When I first read a small note somewhere about Tycho Brahe, I thought that the author was pulling my leg. No one with such a great legacy in scientific history could have been such an insane lunatic. I was wrong.

Tycho was from the super wealthy, elitist class of his day. He was born a twin, but his brother died at birth. Tycho was then kidnapped by his childless uncle, Joergen Brahe, who was the vice admiral to Frederick II. His parents couldn't get Tycho back from uncle Joergen because Joergen was too rich and too powerful.

At school Tycho showed an interest in mathematics, astronomy and astrology. He got his nose all bent out of shape in an argument with a relative and fellow student about who was the best at mathematics. They had a duel and his cousin slashed off his nose. He had an artificial nose constructed out of a sliver and gold alloy that he wore for the rest of his life.

He got exceedingly interested in star gazing and eventually became the leading observational astronomer of his day and maybe ever. He made detailed lists of the movements of the stars and the planets about the heavens. He disagreed with Aristotle on his sphere theory. Aristotle had this notion about fixed and moveable spheres. The area of space beyond the moon was supposedly fixed. Brahe had tracked comets and other things, moving in the suggested fixed areas.

He also didn't like the notions of Copernicus. In Copernicus' notion he could find no stellar parallax (whatever that is) and Copernicus' ideas were not in tune with the scriptures. The scriptures said that the earth was the center of the universe. Tycho re-designed the universe with the earth once again at the center and the sun revolving around it. Copernicus, Tycho and Galileo all agreed on the notion that everything moved in Godly circles. This was one of Pythagoras' mystical notions.

Frederick II liked Tycho so much that he gave him a whole island filled with people. Tycho was mean and nasty and ruled the island like a tyrant. He even had a dwarf slave named Jepp who spent most of his time living under Tycho's dinner table trying to catch some fallen scraps. Tycho ruled over this island paradise until Frederick II croaked and Christian IV took over.

25

Christian wasn't about to put up with Tycho and his wicked, wicked ways. But Tycho was immediately picked up by the Roman Emperor Rudolph II who gave him Benatek Castle near Prague.

It was while at this castle that Brahe contacted Johannes Kepler. Brahe had heard about Kepler and he wanted him as his assistant. They ended up becoming the Laurel and Hardy or the Martin and Lewis of astronomical history. It was a good financial opportunity for Kepler but their personalities didn't jive. Brahe was drunken, abusive and secretive. He didn't like "sharing" very much. Nevertheless, when he died he left all of his heavenly calculations to Kepler. He died in a rather fitting manner.

One evening he had an important house guest. Brahe was busy over-eating and over-drinking. Brahe, being true to class tradition, refused to leave the table before his guest did. Consequently, he never got to go to the bathroom. This caused him a urinary infection that killed him.

In any case, he left Kepler all of his astronomical records and calculations. Information that Brahe's family didn't really want to give up, but finally did. Brahe's last words with Kepler at his bedside were, supposedly, "Let me not seem to have lived in vain."

Giordano Bruno (1548-1600)

Giordano Bruno's major claim to fame was his ultimate demise. He was sentenced to death by the Roman Catholic Church. On February 19, 1600, he had a wedge stuck into his mouth and was put to death in what was considered a most "humane" and painless manner. He was burnt to death at the stake.

This does make one wonder what was considered at that time to be an inhumane and painful death. I'm sure we don't want to find out, do we?

For some reason no one likes to say that the Roman Catholic Church was prone to killing and torturing people to death in those days. Most historians use the euphemism of *The Inquisition*. "*The Inquisition* made me do it." It was the Roman Catholic Church who did it.

Fortunately for us the Roman Catholic Church has had some minor changes in policy since those good old days. You can still be condemned as a heretic and sentenced to death and punishment, but the enforcement of this judgment is left to God and the torture to an eternity in hell.

Getting tortured tomorrow in someone's imagination even for an eternity, I like a lot better than having my toenails pulled out this afternoon. But, before all you Protestants start feeling holy, Calvinists in Geneva, and Lutherans in Germany and holy people most everywhere else were doing much the same type thing to the atheists and heretics in their neighborhood.

What did Bruno say to get himself fried? Well, he claimed that the universe was infinite. He said that God was infinite too, though. He even went so far as to say that God was even more infinite than the universe was infinite. The universe was more like finitely infinite, where as God was infinitely infinite. The universe, you see, is made up of an infinity of finite things. God, on the other hand, is contained infinitely even in the finite.

Boy, you should think that type double-speak would have got him off the hook. Unfortunately, he also came to the conclusion that Jesus was not divine and that Copernicus was actually more correct about the sun and the movement of the planets than Ptolemy. Aristotle and his unmoved mover didn't really move him all that much. He also believed in magic and Voodoo and stuff like that. He thought that Jesus might in fact have been a magician.

He is credited to have been an inspiration for Galileo, who showed up about thirty-three years later. He was an example Galileo didn't want to follow. Supposedly Spinoza, Leibniz and even the novelist James Joyce, with his Bruno Nolan in *Finnegan's Wake,* had been exposed to Giordano Bruno.

Bruno was from the town of "Nola" near Naples in Italy. He believed that all of matter had an animate inner being that made it move. Movement needed no external motivation or motivator. I suppose someone could look at this notion as inspiration for Newton's theory of gravity, or Galileo's - a body in motion tends to remain in motion; and later, Einstein's scientific notions with regards to magnetism and relativity.

Bruno though, unlike Einstein, believed space was real and infinite. This type thinking also made Bruno somewhat the granddaddy of Spinozian pantheism. His acceptance of the notion of God being infinitely actual and lacking in potential supposedly helped Leibniz develop his "this is the best of all possible worlds" theory. Bruno liked writing in dialogues like Plato, but seemed to have a much better sense of humor.

Carneades   (c 213 - 128 BC)

Carneades was a skeptic and, at one time, head of Plato's New Academy. Carneades was born in Cyrene, Cyrenaica - now a part of what we know as Libya. He went blind in his old age and is said to have lived until about eighty-five years of age. He wasn't much of a believer in the "clothes make the man" theory. He dressed "negligently." I understand that to mean he was a slob. He wasn't much for McDonald's either. It is claimed that he never accepted a dinner invitation; he was always too busy - thinking. Even when he fed himself at home he had problems. He concentrated so greatly on what he was thinking that he had trouble finding his mouth with his hands. It is said that some of his friends had to move his arms for him. He did a lot of thinking but not much writing - if he did write anything nobody has been able to find it. Most of what we know of Carneades comes to us via Sextus Empericus and Cicero.

He went to Rome in about 156 B.C. to try and get Athens out from a fine that had been imposed. While he was there he decided to give a couple of lectures. In his first lecture he expounded the views of Aristotle and Plato on justice. In his second lecture he refuted, with equal vigor, everything he had said in his first lecture. His point was to show that no matter what point of view you have it isn't warranted. To argue both sides of any argument was a Carnaedesian trademark.

Carnaedes believed that exact truth was indiscernible. As humans we can only approximate a probable truth. Even our sense experiences are lacking and can only supply us with approximation and probabilities. He precedes David Hume in his skeptical analysis of causes and causation.

In theology he challenged the credibility of the concept of God or the Gods. He argued that the powers and activities assigned to divine beings are not consistent with their being changeless and eternal; that the evils in the universe are not consistent with divine providence; that the occurrence of accidental designs, for example, a rock that has the form of a head, invalidates the argument that a design implies a designer; that no clear boundary can be drawn between what is divine and what is not divine; consensus gentium (agreement of the clans – argumentum ad populum) "Everybody believes in God therefore God must exist." Carnaedes said the existence of atheists and nations that know nothing about God(s) disprove the notion that something is true because everybody believes it. Also belief may be universal but remain incorrect. A personal God need not be necessary to have created the universe and the things within it - nature could have formed them herself. If God is both infinite and unlimited, he would fill the universe but be unable to move. A God that would be incapable of movement would be limited. Therefore an unlimited, infinite God is impossible. God is defined as virtuous and perfect. Virtue implies overcoming both pain and danger and only for a being who can suffer or be destroyed are there pains and dangers. Neither suffering nor destructibility is consistent with perfection. God can not be both virtuous and perfect. If God is provident how can he allow so many men to use their reason faultily and in a way injurious to themselves and others? Moreover if he allows weaknesses and misery in the universe - whether intentionally or unintentionally - he is at fault, since intentional or unintentional neglect are both faults.

Carnaedes not only precedes Hume with regards to causation but Sartre with regards to freewill. The will may be caused but it is caused by itself and moves by virtue of its own nature. Events precede a man's action, but do not force him to act. A man's will always has the last move. Carnaedes obviously forgot to ask from whence this freewill came and at what point in a human's existence was it incorporated. Do babies have it, do adolescents have it; do teenagers have it; do monkey and cats and dogs have it?

In general he taught that: Correct information about reality is impossible; truth does not exist, only degrees of probability; probability is the only guide to life; some beliefs can be rated as more probable than others; the higher that probability, the greater the chances of our belief being acted upon correctly; the more probable our belief, the more we should tend to accept it. Bottom line - one does not need objective truth to act but only a probable understanding.

I don't know, I guess - he's probably right, I suppose.

Nicolaus Copernicus (1473 -1543)

Nicolaus Copernicus was a Polack in denial. It seems that he would rather have been a German. But there is no recorded historical documentation confirming the notion that Copernicus ever roamed about the streets of his hometown, Thorn on the Vistula, telling dumb Polack jokes. Whether he was proud of it or not, he was born in Polish territory to a Polish father who was born in Cracow. For some reason none of the biographies that I've read seem to want to mention his mother. I'll bet she was Jewish or Muslim or something and nobody wants to admit it.

Nicolaus was obviously a lazy S.O.B. who didn't want to get a real job. He spent most of his life sucking a free education out of the Roman Catholic Church. He went to school for about twenty seven darn years. First he studied mathematics, then astronomy, and finally he got off the pot and became a doctor. I'll bet his mom and dad were happy - though they were probably dead by that time.

Nicolaus, besides being a lazy screw-off who didn't want to work and sucked up one scholarship after another for his FREE perpetual education, wasn't really much of a hero either. He had discovered, early on in his free education in math and astronomy that the earth wasn't really the center of the universe. He figured out that the earth was actually moving on it axis and in orbit around the sun. So, does he tell anybody about it? Hell no. He sits on the darn information until he is just about to croak. Why? Because he was afraid to get locked in his room for life or get his little tootsies toasted by the Pope and the Inquisition.

The Church had declared that this guy named Ptolemy who had compiled a book that he called the *Almagest*, which he basically gleaned and plagiarized from nearly everybody in the scientific world who came before him, was the sole authority on the subject. Ptolemy's notion that the earth didn't move and everything else did, supposedly confirmed some story in the Bible. Since the Bible was "the revealed word of God," Ptolemy had to be right and everybody else wrong.

Ptolemy's version of the universe, or at least our little part of it, had Jupiter and Mars doing hook shots and fast breaks to the right and the left all about the heavens. Nobody at the time had a problem with this because, as many people still contend today - if that's the way God wants it to be, that is the way it will be, by golly.

Copernicus used his trigonometry and his geometry and his astronomy to point out that if the earth were really moving, all of these planetary shenanigans would be logically explainable and confirmable mathematically. Copernicus got his *De revolutionibus* published on his death bed in 1543 and in just a few short years later, 1838 or so, the Catholic Church finally agreed with him. I don't know about you, but that certainly gives me hope with regards to the Catholic point of view on birth control, abortion, pedophilia and women as priests.

Copernicus was a "liberal." Worse than that, he was a "humanist." And the conservatives of his day have Anna Schillings to prove it. What did a sixty-five year old, like Copernicus, need a pretty, little, twenty year old housekeeper like Anna for, anyway? Besides, Copernicus stole most of what he had to say from Plato, Philalaus, and Aristarchus. Liberals, ha! They're all the same.

Charles Darwin (1809-1882)

Charles Darwin's *Origins of the Species* started a rumble heard around the world. His research started a turn of events that I am sure he never imagined. His ideas oozed out into not only science and biology but economics, politics, philosophy, sociology, religion, theology and history.

Karl Marx thought of himself as an evolutionist. He felt that he had discovered, much like Darwin in biology, a process behind the advancement of civilization which was triggered and had as its root in economics and the resulting distinctions of class. He even asked Darwin if he could dedicate his *Das Kapital* to him. Darwin declined the privilege. Marx and subsequent followers felt that this natural and inevitable process could be stimulated and prematurely advanced by the interjection of active physical revolution.

Hegel theorized an evolutionary connection in the philosophical and historical advancement in the world of ideas, and social thought. He saw the evolution of thought stemming from a process of intellectual argumentation advanced through a system of thesis, antithesis, and eventual synthesis, which he attempted to prove and substantiate through the study of history.

Adolf Hitler takes Darwin to new heights or should I say depths. He uses Darwin and Hegel, couples them with a sort of aristocratic/individualistic elitism and develops a cruel but consistent form of social Darwinism. In his theory of social development he contrives the notion that the process of the survival of the fittest is not only inevitable but obligatory. And he, as one of the world's fittest, decides to rid the world of its unfit. He would use the weapons of population control practiced by Mother Nature and advanced in the theories of the Reverend Malthus - adding to the Malthusian list of war, disease, and famine, outright extermination and genocide. He establishes the legitimacy of these tactics from his observations of Mother Nature, Divine Providence and human history, making reference to such "greats" as Alexander, Frederick, Attila and the Holy Roman Empire.

Contrary to popular opinion Adolf Hitler is the antithesis of Karl Marx who predicted the eventual rise of the masses into a pure democratic state fostered by the abuses of the monopolistic, destructively competitive, over-productive tendencies of the industrial revolution.

Darwin, I am sure, would never have predicted that his ideas would have led to such catastrophe, much the same as Jesus Christ would never have fathomed medieval Christianity, nor Albert Einstein and the Cures, Hiroshima and Nagasaki.

Albert Einstein, (1879-1955)

$E = MC^2$

This equation showing a relationship between energy and mass or matter is everywhere. I see T-shirts and dolls and hats and placards, and notebooks and posters and calendars and whatever with this equation or the man responsible, plastered onto it wherever I go. Whenever I see these ads, I wonder if the people wearing, holding or displaying them know what a controversial and plagued life the discoverer of this equation lived.

When Albert first proposed his equation and Special Theory on Relativity he was denounced from every corner of the scientific community. He was called everything from a fool to a mad man.

Because of his scientific inclinations he was denounced as an atheist by most of the conventional, religious community throughout the world.

He believed in democracy but was also an advocate of socialism which put him at odds with most of the free capitalist world.

He renounced his citizenship to the country in which he was born. He was not only a hater of his country's authoritarianism, anti-Semitism, and Nazism, but he was a staunch opponent to the notion of organized militarism, anywhere. He had nothing but disrespect for soldiering and men who would lockstep behind one another in parades, and follow orders that challenged even their own conscience. He went so far as to champion an organization after World War I that encouraged young men all over the world to refuse to serve in the militaries of their nations - the theory being that if all young men refused to serve in their nation's militaries, this would be the end to war.

He escaped anti-Semitic Germany and Europe through the magnanimity of a wealthy lover of learning, the philanthropist Louis Bamberger.

Mr. Bamberger founded a department store in Newark, New Jersey which he later sold to Macy and Company. He shared a million dollars of the sale with 240 of his faithful employees.

Bamberger and his sister established the School for Advanced Studies at Princeton University and Albert Einstein was nominated as its first department head.

Albert Einstein was not welcomed to Princeton or the U.S. with a tickertape parade. In fact, he was greeted at dockside by women and mothers carrying signs labeling him as a Godless traitor and a coward - primarily, because of his pacifistic and anti-militarist positions.

From what I can see because of his political and religious inclinations, Albert Einstein spent the remainder of his life pretty much hiding out at Princeton.

When asked to be the first leader of the new country of Israel he nearly had a heart attack while talking on the phone. Albert had gotten his fill of public notoriety, and who could blame him.

He sent a famous letter to FDR warning about Germany and the possible threat of a nuclear or atomic bomb. Although Albert was a lover of peace, Adolf Hitler was even too much for Albert to swallow.

When Albert was on his death bed he was asked if he was afraid to die. He suggested that with his knowledge of the universe and observing Mother Nature from out his window, he saw nothing to fear.

I'm still looking out the window at Mother Nature and she certainly doesn't look harmless to me. Maybe Albert had a special, magic window or something – like Alice's looking glass. What was he seeing out that window that brought him peace and tranquility, I wonder?

Epicurus (342-270 BC)

Epicurus was not an "epicurean." He believed that in life man should seek happiness and pleasure, but yet he ate only bread and water, an occasional piece of dried cheese and a sip of wine, and didn't have sex.

He didn't like eating because it caused indigestion, drinking led to a hangover, and sex led to passion, frustration and, least we should forget, children.

He didn't like politics because expressing a political point of view led to the creation of enemies and if one is to be happy one should only have friends.

He believed in God, or the Gods, and liked going to church. Supposedly he worshipped daily and was considered devoutly religious, yet he hated and despised religion because it promoted mysticism, superstition, fear, and barbaric human sacrifices. He believed in the Gods but realized that if the Gods were to remain happy they had to ignore mankind. A good point, don't you agree?

The Gods didn't control anything and atoms acted independently often without rhyme or reason. Chaos ruled the universe and not design or divine planning. Because of this notion Epicurus is basically considered an atheist.

He is criticized on two counts by believers. One, he gives no account of consciousness or an explanation of how unconscious matter can produce conscious thought. And two, if random atoms or particles, chaotically bumping into one another are the building blocks of man and his universe, who or what sets them or keeps them in motion? How can anything revolve without a Revolver?

But do we have an answer to either of these questions today? What is the source of consciousness, reflection, thought?

No one knows.

And what is the source of motion?

Gravity and electromagnetism are simply possible descriptions of the movement as observed, but the cause or the source of the motion as of yet has not been determined.

Those that posit the Big Bang Theory, as an explanation of the motion of the universe still have the problem of explaining the source of the energy causing the Big Bang to bang. And those that posit God still have the age old problem of answering from whence came God, his power, consciousness and energy?

From what I can see "conscious thought" is really no cause for divination. Human consciousness seems to me to be a most primitive, elementary, and imperfect a process of understanding that only the immense ego of man could assign to the ranks of the Godly. Even our so called scientific method when viewed objectively must appear to any conscious observer like a poor ram butting his head up against the dam, or a spider reconstructing his bridge from wall to wall, over and over and over. Man's inductive process of learning is mighty slow. Computers have already surpassed most of us and who knows what the future has instore?

Epicurus was a poor guy, unlike Plato and Aristotle. He started up his school in what appears to have been a bad neighborhood. He took into his school a lot of local riffraff, for which he has received endless bad mouthing.

I don't understand schools of philosophy in ancient Athens and Greece. Everybody and his uncle had one. I picture these schools to be on every street corner, like barrooms in South Boston, or independent churches throughout the South.

What was the deal on this?

Sigmund Freud (1856-1939)

Sigmund Freud is listed in every book of great modern-day thinkers. Freud's area of discovery was the human mind. Trying to figure out what it is that he actually discovered is not so easy. His discovery with regards to the human mind is called Psychoanalysis. Via processes and techniques, Freud tried to analyze how the human mind functioned. How it worked. How a human being actually thinks. Today his ideas are so commonplace in all of our lives that it is impossible to imagine that there was a time when these ideas were not known and accepted.

If you want to know what makes your husband tick, for example. You will want to know what his parents were like; what kind of a childhood he had; what his education was; what kind of company he kept; what books he read; what his aspirations are; what his fears are; what his hopes, dreams, idiosyncrasies, and peculiarities are; what he believes in; what his religion is; what the social mores and customs of his native land are. Who does he admire? Who does he hate? We can go on and on, and it all seems like plain, old common sense. Yet, this is all Freudian. It's called psychoanalysis. It's sublimation and repression and sub-conscious and conscious. It's association. It's transference. It's ego and id and super ego. Even a misplaced word or slip of the tongue could be defined as Freudian. The influences of our sexuality on our ways of thinking, our conclusions and actions, is all Freudian.

So how did we analyze the workings of the human mind before Freud? I don't know. And what is worse, I can't even imagine. Today many people tell us that Freud was wrong.

About what?

Freud was interested in the human mind; in diseases that were the product of mental processes and not physical conditions within the body. He was interested in dreams and their reason and origin in the human mind. When he expressed many of his fundamental theories and discoveries, he was literally laughed at by the medical community of his day. He discovered that many mental illnesses were an exaggeration of normal inhibitions, fears or aspirations.

He studied hysteria and hypnotism under a doctor named Charcot. He worked on his dream theories with Carl Jung. He proposed theories like the Oedipus Complex. This Complex suggested that a child has a tendency to fall in love with the parent of the opposite sex and harbors feeling of competition and resentment towards the parent of the same sex. My personal theory is that a child has a tendency to like people who treat him kindly and tends to dislike people who treat him unkindly. This goes for parents as well as strangers. In fact, the child oftentimes can't tell one from the other.

Freud theorized that even small children had a sexual nature. I feel that sex comes to most of us somewhat suddenly and is quite a shock. We learn a little more about it from friends, neighbors, relatives and parents, after which, we give some form of it a try, and then can't stop doing it. During this compulsive period we justify our neurotic, psychotic, irrational, perverted antics in every possible way. When suddenly the urge dissipates and we wake up, we can hardly believe that we were ever inclined to behave in such a manner. We try to guide our children and the rest of mankind according to our new, more mature awaking. It doesn't seem to be working.

Galileo Galilei (1564-1642)

Okay, say this guy's name aloud, three times and say it fast.

All right! Now you know how to yodel. Didn't think you could do it, did you?

Galileo is another one of those guys who just didn't know what to do with himself. His father wanted him to be a traveling salesman, peddling cloth. Galileo wanted to be either a scientist or a mathematician. They compromised and Galileo went to medical school in Pisa. Even in those days doctors made good money. You could make pretty good money at math or science, if you also played the bass fiddle and could moonlight on the weekends with the Dave Brubeck Quartet.

Anyway, this seemed like a good compromise to Galileo's father, but junior had other ideas. Instead of reading his Hippocrates and Galen, he kept sneaking in dirty books with pictures in them, drawn by Euclid and Archimedes. There was no Playboy or Hustler in those days. You just had to take whatever figures you could get. Needless to say, Galileo flunked out of medical school. But reading all his dirty books did land him a professor's job at the University. No money, but a professor. Whoopee!

Well, besides everything else, Galileo was a hippie. He refused to wear his toga when he was off duty. He probably had green hair and an earring too. He had a big problem with authority. He kept bad-mouthing Aristotle. Mr. Aristotle, the poor guy, was dead too.

Aristotle was the last word on everything intellectual in those days. It didn't matter whether he was right or wrong. "Magister Dixit," everybody said. "The master has spoken." That was it. The next thing you know, there's Galileo dropping bowling balls off the leaning tower of Pisa for the sole purpose of trying to make the master look dopey. That and a few other antics and they finally fired Galileo's butt.

Then, believe it or not, he falls into a great job at the University of Padua. Talk about luck! Everybody in Padua loves the guy. But Galileo just can't stand all the success. He blows all his paychecks, gets into debt up to his ears, and has a local prostitute move into his apartment with him. Her name is

Maria Gamba. She has three kids by him and who knows how many by everybody else. His dad must have just loved this.

In any case, he starts playing his lute around town at the local dives to earn a couple of bucks. He invents a compass and a telescope, but because he more than likely slept during marketing class, he can't make a buck on either of them. Next he gets a book published, *Sidereus Nuncius* (*the Messenger of the Stars*) in which he casually mentions that he has been watching all the planets revolve around the sun with his new telescope. Sounds harmless enough, except that in those days the planets didn't revolve around the sun; the sun and the planets revolved around the earth. How did they know that? Easy, Magister Dixit. Even this would have been okay, if the dufus didn't go and decide to move back to Pisa.

At Pisa, they put him on trial for bad mouthing "the Master." They force him to swear on a stack of Bibles that the earth does not revolve around the sun. He spends the rest of his life in prison, as opposed to being burnt at the stake, on condition that he writes no more books.

Yup, you guessed it. His next, and last, book was entitled *The Laws of Motion*. And he couldn't even read it. He went blind in his prison cell in Arcetri trying to write the darn thing. Some guys just don't know when to quit.

Laplace (1749-1827)

Pierre Simon Laplace was a mathematician and astronomer. He was a poor boy from a peasant background. He seems to have had a knack for kissing-up and getting people to like him. This trait got his neighbors to pay to educate him and helped him to succeed in a political career in very perilous times. He was a brilliant scientist but, nevertheless, always willing to steal material from any source.

After his rise from peasant-hood, he succeeded to what most biographers have characterized as a snob. He hid his background and treated even old benefactors shabbily. He is renowned as the most famous and outspoken atheist of his day. When criticized by Napoleon Bonaparte for never mentioning God in his famous work on the heavens, *Mecanique Celeste,* he is recorded to have answered that he had no need for such a hypothesis.

After Lavoisier got his head chopped off in the Revolution, Laplace and Lagrange saved their necks by slipping into the now vacant position at the national powder works. When Napoleon came to power, Laplace once again ingratiated himself into a cushy government job as secretary of the interior. He didn't last there long but was soon bounced, conveniently, into another governmental department. By the time Louis XVIII came along he had a seat in the Chamber of Peers and was now the Marquis de Laplace.

He is acclaimed by some to be the Isaac Newton of France. His *Mecanique Celeste* is, in fact, a translation of Newton's *Principia* into the language of infinitesimal calculus and a completion of Newton ideas in many details. It may have been his attention to such details that gave him the confidence to counter Newton's need for an occasional intervening God. Where Newton needed God as a final explanation, Laplace had mathematical and physical facts.

Laplace is also noted for stating that with enough physical science, principles and knowledge of the universe, a superior intellect would not only be capable of reconstructing the heavenly past but could also predict the future of the universe. So now along with his being classified an atheist, Laplace was also considered a determinist. I suppose the inference here is that if one felt that the future of the stars was predictable then so too would be the future of mankind. I don't see the connection, but what do I know.

Whether or not M. Laplace was a good guy or a bad guy seems to depend on who you talk to. But, that he was a smart guy goes without question.

At eighteen he applied for a job to d'Alembert, the famous mathematician and Encyclopedist. Laplace brought with him a recommendation, yet d'Alembert refused to see him. Laplace then wrote him a letter on the general principles of mechanics. Laplace got the position. Mr. d'Alembert obviously believed that it was not who you know but what you know that counted.

Laplace re-established Kant's nebular hypothesis stating that the solar system evolved from gases rotating around the sun. The gases formed rings which then cooled and formed the planets.

He not only illuminated every branch of physics with his "Laplace equations" but did lasting work in the theory of probabilities. He calculated the earth's dynamical ellipticity. He developed an analytical theory of the tides. He deduced the mass of the moon. He improved methods for determining the orbits of comets. In 1798 General Bonaparte even took him to Egypt to study the stars from the top of the Pyramids.

Lucretius   (c 95 - 55 BC)

Everywhere you look through the annals of Philosophic history you will find a little bit about Lucretius - the only problem is that it is usually the same "little bit."

Lucretius' full name was Titus Lucretius Carus. He wrote a famous philosophical, didactic poem entitled *De Rerum Natura* (*On the Nature of Things*). This poem consisted of 7,400 hexameter lines and was divided into six books. According to St. Jerome this poem was composed during the lucid intervals of a madness which was caused by the ingestion of a philtre (love potion) the end result of which was that Lucretius killed himself.

The poem taught, among other things, that there was no need to fear death - obviously Lucretius took this notion to heart. He was just a young man at the time - in his mid forties (44?). And that seems to be it as far as the documented evidence about Lucretius goes.

But even the documented is not taken as absolute. It is hard to believe for many dedicated to the study of philosophy, reading what Lucretius says in book 4 about women and physical love, that he would be drinking a love potion. Nor are many students capable of accepting that this great philosophic poem was the ranting of the insane or the writing of a man in delirium. Some suggest that the whole story is a slander to defame Lucretius for his irreligiosity.

As far as the uncorroborated evidence goes, he seems to have been from a good Roman family and fairly well educated. He may have been a friend of Gaius Memmius - a Roman statesman. It is rumored that he kept to himself, maybe even living as somewhat of a recluse.

His famous poem is meant to be an interpretation of the ideas and philosophy of the famous Greek materialistic (atomist) philosopher Epicurus. But since not all that much is known about Epicurus, Lucretius gets high marks for his interpretive rethinking of the great Greek materialist.

Interesting to note, Epicurus didn't like poets or poetry. In fact Epicurus felt that "a wise man would not write poetry" and certainly not while drinking a "philter." A martini or a Manhattan probably would have sufficed and possibly the ill effects and the end result could have been avoided. Even two or three martinis might have left Lucretius with a slight hangover - but at least he would have been ... leftover.

Lucretius may also have been a war resister. He was not partial to militarism or the Roman idea of duty to the State (the Roman Draft). This was not a popular idea or position in the Roman Empire. Actually it wasn't all that popular among the Greeks either. The Romans were big on Law but they did not have a chapter of the ACLU in the whole Empire. So maybe killing himself wasn't all that tragic - he could have ended up nailed to a cross along the Appian Way dying of thirst and starvation.

Lucretius is in some quarters snidely criticized as possibly being a pantheist. A pantheist is described by critics to be a sort of lunatic who prays at the foot of a Walnut or Spruce tree out in the woods rather than ascribing to the ego-maniacal, anthropological concept that the universe was actually created by a super-human type entity who is more often than not described as a cross between Charles Atlas and Superman.

In his poem Lucretius states that in the beginning there were atoms and vacuous space and all that is, results somehow from the interaction, random and wayward motion of these two quantities. If we interpret "motion" to be energy, we find ourselves not so far from what is accepted as the scientific cosmology of today - in fact it may be even closer to the cosmology of tomorrow. We will just have to wait and see.

When Lucrecius leaves the area of cosmology and gets into sensation and perception we vacate the area of precocious futuristic genius and enter the realm of the pre-scientific Platonic and Aristotelian misdirection. But when we emerge once again in the *Ethics* we find ourselves in the never-never land of genius, insight, and thoughtful contemplation. One could spend a great deal of time, indeed, pondering over the ethical passages in Lucretius' poem.

Isaac Newton (1642-1727)

Isaac had a rough start. His father died before he was born, and his mother dumped him on the relatives and ran off and married a minister. This may explain why Isaac never married and supposedly died a virgin.

How anyone could possibly know that Isaac died a virgin is beyond me. But I have read this now in several Isaac Newton biographies. So, take it for what it is worth. I have searched Amazon for a book entitled *My Secret Affair with Isaac Newton*, but I've found nothing.

Isaac was a very religious child and a defender and seeker of religious inspiration throughout his life. In fact, it is my personal opinion that Isaac, like Thomas Aquinas and many other true believers before him, actually devoted his life to proving or trying to prove the existence of God. In fact, I think that Isaac's *Principia* and its consequent description of the forces of gravity, is his attempt at establishing God's existence.

To Isaac, God had cast the stars and planets into space by hand (space being another attribute of God himself) and then manipulated their course through this Godly space by emanating an unexplainable, mystical, controlling power that Isaac named, gravity.

He went on to prove that there was such a controlling, manipulative mystical power. He derived, mathematically, the orbits of planets, stars, comets, the moon and even the tides on earth, according to this unexplainable, unseen force called gravity. To Isaac gravity was the invisible guiding hand of God constantly at work keeping everything, rotating, making elliptical or predictable orbits, and floating around in space. When asked to further explain this force, Isaac declined. He said that the knowledge of such a Power was sufficient. The fact that he could demonstrate, mathematically, the physical effects of such a force was proof enough that such a force existed. Isaac had proved, at least to himself, through the "fact" of gravity that there was a God.

Strangely enough, if it weren't for Halley (the Halley of later comet fame) there would, probably, never have been any *Principia*. Halley not only encouraged but paid for the publication of Newton's monumental work.

It is said by many that Isaac Newton may be the brightest man who has ever lived. Yet as an adult, he nearly poked his eye out with a stick while doing an experiment, deflecting light rays through his cornea.

On another occasion, he nearly blinded himself staring at the sun all day. This was an experiment with light. He was seeking a pattern in the spots appearing before his eyes.

Finally he ended up having a nervous breakdown. Some suspect, caused by his habit of identifying chemicals used in his "Alchemy" experiments by tasting them.

He was a religious enthusiast to the last. He spent his old age, analyzing the Bible, and writing *A Short Scheme of the True Religion* - a failing attempt which he wrote and re-wrote to prove the essence and truth of religion.

But with all his Biblical endeavors, he did not believe in the Trinity, or in the divinity of Jesus, nor in the authority of the Church. He held the Lucasian Chair at Trinity College, Cambridge, England. The Lucasian Chair (Mathematics honor) was established in 1663 by Henry Lucas and made official by King Charles II in 1664.

Newton was also elected to Parliament, and appointed Warden of the Mint of England.

I don't know, but between nearly poking his eye out with a stick, alchemy and never having sex, he certainly couldn't have been all that bright. So he liked math! Is that any reason to make the guy a knight, I ask you?

Blaise Pascal (1623-1662)

Blaise Pascal was a child prodigy, a mathematical genius. In his teens he is credited with discovering geometry on his own, and inventing an adding machine - the first such "machine" ever in history. He also formulated the laws of probability. But in all "probability," Blaise was most probably a psychological whacko. He was extremely self-abusive. Nearing the end of his rather short life of thirty-nine years, he actually tortured himself with contrived devices. He believed that man's purpose in life was to suffer and then to die. And if death doesn't come soon enough it would behoove a "good" man to seek it out, I suppose. I say he was a whack-o; he claimed to be nothing more than a good Christian.

He had a big problem with affection. He wouldn't hug anybody, not even his sister's children. He admonished his sister for calling another woman beautiful. He told his sister never to say such things again for she knew not what evil thoughts she might be inspiring in others. I think that if Blaise would have had a flame light in his heart for maybe a little Rose or a Gertrude, he might have come to a much better understanding of the science and probable predictions of hugging and he probably would have led a much happier life.

Another of his achievements in the realm of thought is his development of what is called Pascal's wager. He said that if it came to a choice in your mind of believing in God or not believing in God, you should place your bet on belief in God; because believing provides an opportunity for heaven, while not believing provides only nothingness or hell.

Yes, but I would add that if you are prone to take such a calculating attitude, you should go a step further, and take the choice of Hinduism over Christianity. At least with the God of Hinduism you are offered more than one fleeting, confusing chance at life to determine the moral truth of this existence. I might also add that if given the choice of one confusing episode with life determining one's fate for a possible eternity of endless suffering in hell, I would think that the most of us, even given our basic impetuousness, would never take such a gamble, and thus a rational human race would never have been born.

Plato (428-347 BC)

Plato was a little, rich boy. Like a lot of other little, rich boys, he thought that he knew it all (think of William F. Buckley). If you believe in democracy, and the ideals of equality, and the principles on which the American Constitution is based, Plato is NOT your main man. In fact, most of the criticisms of democratic life and the democratic political system that were spewed out of the mouth of Adolf Hitler centuries later, were first laid down by Plato in his *Dialogues*, or his attempt at Utopian thinking, *The Republic*.

Plato was an aristocratic, elitist, totalitarian type who was run out of the country after his mentor Socrates was given his poison potion. Socrates was given his choice of poison potion or exile but basically chose to kill himself. He was old anyway, and his wife drove him nuts. Socrates liked (interpreting the writing of Plato) to get all of the little, rich boys in the neighborhood riled up about their personal greatness and superiority over the common, democratic, mediocre schmuck.

Plato's uncle, Critias, was the leader of an oligarchic party of wealthy elitist who preached against the Athenian Democracy, and established, for a very short period, one of the cruelest dictatorships of the period. When the Democracy was restored, Socrates was arrested. He was tried and found guilty of a lesser crime. He side-stepped a granted amnesty and his buddy Plato ran for the hills.

Plato traveled around the world for about twelve years talking to Kings and Queens, other little, rich boys and dictator sorts everywhere.

After things calmed down, he returned home and began re-agitating the system by way of education. He was being permitted that option from the privilege granted under a "democratic" system - the type of agitation that would certainly not have been permitted under the reign of his uncle, Critias.

Plato is most famous for his *Allegory of the Cave* in which he explains to us that our real existence is actually imaginary, and our imaginary existence is true reality. If you like Plato, you will love Descartes. You might also go on to cultivate an interest in Voodoo, witchcraft, and Black Magic.

Plato was really a dramatist and playwright. His *Dialogues* are basically plays. They are masterpieces of developmental logic, and often mis-logic. I loved reading the *Dialogues*, but pretty much gave up reading Plato after wallowing through The *Republic*.

Plato, like Confucius, got the opportunity to try out some of his political ideas. He nearly got himself killed by Dionysius of Syracuse, who then, had a change of heart and simply sold Plato into slavery. He was released and returned home by a benefactor who had purchased him.

At eighty-one he fell asleep in a corner at a party and didn't wake up.

Pythagoras
(530-570 BC ?)

Pythagoras, more than anything else, was a religious leader. He started a secret society and neither he nor any of its members wrote any books about it. Everything we have on Pythagoras is a hand-me-down from somebody else - Plato and Aristotle in particular. If we say that Jesus was interested in morals and Moses was interested in laws and Buddha in sociology, Pythagoras was interested in numbers. He was the mathematician and scientific mind of the religious right of his day.

Pythagoras was an Ionian Greek, born on the island of Samos between 530 B.C. and 570 B.C. Everybody has an estimate of when he was born but no one seems to care very much about when or if he ever died. I will presume that he did die at some time. But, as with all religious leaders, Pythagoras started a movement that lived centuries beyond his personal lifespan. What we know or understand of the movement today may or may not be representative of Pythagoras, as with the other religious leaders. But, nevertheless, he gets the blame or the credit depending on your point of view.

Many writers credit Plato's mysticism and "theory of ideas" and the Demiurge to Pythagoras, others add Euclid's geometry, many add Copernicus, Kepler and Tycho Brache's cosmologies, and some even go so far as to include Einstein and Relativity. Honestly, to me, this guy sounds like another religious wacko.

He supposedly advised his followers not to eat meat or beans, not to walk in the main street of town, not to stand on your nail clippings, not to draw pictures in ashes and don't sit on a bushel basket.

With numbers he really went into orbit. Numbers were fundamental and real. They represented shapes - hence, our notions today of numbers to the square or the cube. He brought his mathematics and numbers into his religion and took his religion into his politics. I don't know what his politics were but they must have been serious because other folks killed, burnt and chased his followers out of Kroton in southern Italy, and then out of Italy entirely.

He also connected his numbers to music. He felt that the planets and all the moving bodies in space were making music. We can't hear it because we are so much conditioned to this celestial noise that we no longer notice it. He believed in the soul and in its transmigration. He once counseled a friend to stop beating his dog because he heard in its yelping the voice of an old friend.

I can understand the logic in the transmigration of souls but then why the emphasis on the contemplation and meditation and perfection of our own divine transmigrating soul? I mean, if you are going to be a dog or a rat in your next life, what's to think about?

Copleston states that Pythagoras was more interested in establishing a "way of life" rather that a cosmology. Thus Copleston considers him more a religious leader than a philosopher. So, if religion is looking for "the way," and philosophy is looking for "the how," who or what is interested in the "why," I wonder?

Oh Yeah, let's not forget $a^2 + b^2 = c^2$.

The Trial of Socrates – I. F. Stone

My opinion of Socrates (470-399), which, I presume, must have come from my brief inquires into Plato, was that of a moral hero, a man of great principle, who stood up courageously against authoritarianism, and tyranny. He was a philosopher of the noblest type with a deep love and respect for knowledge in its purest state. Not in the farthest reaches of my deepest cynicism had I ever contemplated Socrates as a Nazi or somebody who might be inclined to lead others into the militant revolutionary overthrow of a democratic government.

This never occurred to me even though I was aware that Socrates was a political critic and cynic, living in what came to be known as the greatest democracy of all time. So then why it never occurred to me that Socrates didn't care very much for democracy is rather shocking to me. How many other rather obvious facts of history am I, or have I been, blind to because of personal preferences or prejudices, or just plain lack of objective insight. I always thought that I was insightful and observant but then again there was that introduction to a U.S. Mail Box and a Campbell's soup can a little while back. It is amazing.

I must admit that I did always wonder what that charge of "corrupting the youth" was all about.

In any case, if you would like to read a new and extremely interesting point of view in regards to the legacy and memory of Socrates, I recommend a book written by I.F. Stone, the political writer, who should not be confused with the romantic writer, Irving F. Stone.

I.F. Stone did his homework on his book, *The Trial of Socrates*, even going so far as to make a study of the ancient Greek language. As amusing as it seems that radical critic of American Democracy and its political shenanigans, I.F. Stone, comes to the aid of the Greek Establishment in their condemnation of the "gad-fly" (more appropriately, great big pain in the butt) Socrates.

This is a real eye opener for Socratophiles. I have no doubt that I am going to read it again, and maybe then once again. It is so filled with common sense and historical insights that it makes me just want to slap myself and say wake up!

It is great fun to see not only how un-insightful one can really be, but even more fun to have a spotlight turned onto your groping at the bedroom night table. And speaking of bedrooms and groping, we won't even get into Alcibiades.

Manya Sklodovska (1867-1934)

Manya Sklodovska was just another dumb Polack; one of those inferior Slavic types who would have been executed or worked to death if Adolf Hitler had his druthers. I found out about Manya by way of a secondhand bookstore where I found a tattered worn copy of her life, written by her daughter. This book is no Mommy Dearest. This book written by a daughter about her Mother is inspirational.

Manya had such a propensity to read books as a young girl that her school-teacher parents tried to keep them away from her. Manya was self-sacrificing, an attribute that is much disparaged today. She sacrificed her own educational opportunities to work as a governess and put her siblings through school. When she finally did get her opportunity to learn, she worked so hard and skimped so, even on food in order to buy books that she nearly succumbed in her own ardent efforts.

She was pursued by a quiet, passionate young man, a student of science who was amazed by Manya's scientific understanding. She also excelled in Math. They had a wonderful and lasting relationship until his death in a terrible shocking tragedy. Together, the two of them working with scanty funds in an unheated shed made a discovery that won them the Nobel Prize on December 10th, 1903. In December of 1911 she won her second Nobel Prize - this time in chemistry. Twenty-four years later, in the same hall in Sweden, another of her daughters, Irene won the same award.

During World War I she adapted the discovery of Roentgen, the X-ray, to a Red Cross vehicle and along with her daughter drove across battlefields servicing field hospital surgeons in their attempts to save the wounded. She twice refused the cross of the Legion of Honor claiming that she was only a soldier doing her duty.

She was the first female professor, and the first female head of a science department at the Sorbonne. She established the first institute of science in her native Poland. The list of her accomplishments goes on and on. She is without doubt one of the most amazing woman that I have ever read about. Each time I look at a picture of this great woman, I see in her eyes another not so great dumb Polack, my grandmother, and it makes me proud.

This book is entitled simply Madame Curie and it was written by one of her daughters, Eve Cure. In my opinion, this is a must-read for any young girl today. Don't miss it.

St. Augustine (354-430)

As far as I can see it took a lot of nerve to make Hogie Augie a Saint. It takes equal hyperbole to call this guy a philosopher, but yet there he is.

If you are a man and you had to be re-born a religious in ancient times, you would want to have been born the Holy Hogie Augie. This holy man's big curse in his early life was an infinite erection.

In his *Confessions* he admits to trying to have sex with everything that didn't move or run away from him. He loved the girls. But, having sex with everybody's mother, sister and granddaughter made him feel guilty. He often fell down on his knees and prayed to God to relieve him of this cross. But just before he got up off his knees, he confesses, he would offer this ejaculation:

"But God please don't remove this curse before I have had my fill."

And it seems that Holy Hogie Augie got his fill right up until he was in his thirties or forties, and then one can only presume that he became impotent or his you-know-what fell off.

My problem has always been that if something made me feel guilty, I couldn't do it. If I did do it, some sort of retribution on my part was required. St. Augustine obviously didn't have this problem. He seems to have been like a good many of the Catholic boys that I grew up with. Making a good confession every Friday night was penance enough for them, and then in the week to follow it was fun and games as usual. And if any unfortunate happened to get pregnant, the baby wasn't theirs.

When I think of St. Augustine, who was a rich and prominent individual for all of his life, I presume, I wonder if any of the numerous illegitimate children that he must have left behind in his sexual wake, ever received a check in the mail? Maybe a little card at Christmas time? How about a ballgame once a month? How about a scholarship to Catholic University?

And what about the girls? Some of them must have fallen in love with him? In his confessions does he write even one passage of remorse and sorrow for the lives that he ruined and for the poor tender hearts that he may have broken? A poem, even, about how sorry he was to have hurt poor tender-hearted little Lulu?

He cries about sins that he committed in the crib and goes on for hundreds of pages about stealing an apple, but I don't recollect or have I yet found any mention of breaking any poor girl's heart, or even apology to any known or unknown fatherless child.

No, Hogie Augie spends his redemption here on earth advising evil women to remain virgins and to stop bringing divinely condemned children with the stain of Original Sin on their souls into the world.

Augie paid his earthly debts to his heavenly father, rather than write a check in the here and now to the individuals he owed. I only wish today that American Express would accept the same type payment plan, and then maybe one day I could be a saint too.

Eli Whitney (1765-1825)

If there were no Eli Whitney there may have been no Civil War.

What do you think about that? It does seem rather far-fetched, doesn't it? Eli Whitney, as we all know, invented the Cotton Gin and then became a multi-millionaire, right?

Wrong. The Cotton Gin was one of those simple inventions that once someone saw it, and if that someone were of the mechanical type, he could put one together himself. No sooner did he complete his Cotton Gin than every good-ole boy had one, and was buzzing it out to his cotton plantation. Eli yelled and screamed and sued everybody that he could possibly sue, but never got very much for all his efforts.

But aside from all of this, I am told, that his little invention revived a slave industry that may have been on its way out in America due to the economics of keeping slaves.

To keep a slave healthy and in working condition, cost bucks; and if the slave owner couldn't figure out a way that his slave could make him more than he cost him - them darn slaves had to go. Even poor slave holders, and there were a bunch of them, were getting tired of planting another row of peas for lazy old Amos.

Around the rest of the world, moral indignation was rising against the concept of some people owning some other people. Besides, why have the trouble and upkeep of owning and caring for a slave when you could rent an Irishman or some other starving immigrant by the hour, and you didn't have to worry about where he slept or got his vitamin pills, and if he died he died.

After the Civil War there were black intellectuals and authors who denounced the immorality of replacing bodily, chattel slavery with the even worse moral outrage of wage-slavery.

But, at just about the time that slave owning folk were tiring of maintaining their slaves, Eli invented the Cotton Gin which made having a captured labor force once again a profitable endeavor. Slaves that had been freed were rounded up once again.

Although Eli made very few dollars on his Cotton Gin he eventually made up for the loss by designing a rifle for the government with interchangeable parts. Actually Eli was America's first Henry Ford. He initiated the notion of interchangeable parts and had his rifles put together on an assembly line.

Presidents, Kings and Rulers

John Adams (1735-1826)

President 1797-1801

John Adams was irascible, argumentative, haughty, aristocratic, demanding and domineering. Yet whenever I read about John Adams something about him makes me smile. If it is possible, his actions speak even louder than his words. He was a pompous, rigid authoritarian but a failure as even a school teacher because of his inability to keep the kids in line. He obviously got no respect - the Rodney Dangerfield of the early presidency.

He was a lover of the British and a Loyalist at the core. He was an avid supporter of the Revolution. He was active in politics, but yet always threatening to quit. He was a male, chauvinist pig, but yet he married Abigail Smith, an outspoken, independent feminist of her day. Not only did he marry her but their love affair and devotion to one another is an inspiration to the romantic novelist. In fact, Irving Stone, the famous historical romantic novelist, wrote just such a book.

The Boston Massacre precipitated public outrage and John chose to defend the British soldiers who shot down his countrymen. He truly expected his political career to come to an end with this dastardly deed. But instead the American political constituency admired his courage.

He argued with his wife, Benjamin Franklin, George Washington, Alexander Hamilton, Thomas Jefferson, Thomas Pain, the French, the British, his fellow colonists, just about everybody around but yet somehow ended up, in my mind, as a guy who basically wanted to be liked. He was an intellectual and nobody ever really knew whose side he was on. He was a tough person to deal with but was somehow recognizable of his own faults. He managed to keep Abigail on his side. He re-established his friendship with political arch rival, Thomas Jefferson. He actually got himself elected president of the United States with this aggravating, dominant personality - even if only for one term.

Though harboring a profound fear of an early death, John lived to be ninety. I can just see him at home arguing with

Abigail. In the middle of the huff, like Archie Bunker, he falls into his chair while clutching his chest and cries, "My heart, my heart! Honey, honey, I think I'm dying."

He was the first president to live in the White House. Then came the Alien and Sedition Acts. These laws actually made it a crime to say something derogatory about the president or the country. In 1799 a fellow by the name of John Fries spoke out against a new tax and said, "damn the president, damn the congress, damn the Aristokratz." And along with the women of the neighborhood and pots of boiling water, he chased away the president's tax collectors.

Fries was apprehended, tried, convicted and sentenced to death. Adams went against his own party and granted Mr. Fries a complete pardon. I'm sure he must have been thinking about himself and his own behavior with regards to the British and their Stamp Act. How could he be responsible for putting a man to death for having a big mouth? He was one of the biggest mouths in American History.

During his administration actual fist fights break out in the House of Representatives - democracy in action. Can't you just see all the Loyalists and aristocrats shaking their heads and saying, "Sure, democracy - government by the common man, yeah right! More like pure anarchy."

I guess that things really haven't changed that much, have they?

Alexander the Great (356-323 BC)

Alexander is known as "the Great," according to the prominent historian Will Cuppy, because he killed more people of more different kinds than any other man of his times.

One thing that one should keep in mind when reading about ancient peoples is that the great majority of them and their rulers were out of their ever-loving minds. Alexander was no exception. His father, Philip of Macedonia, was a raving, alcoholic lunatic. He and young Alexander had numerous fist fights, and on several occasions tried to stab one another to death. Dad always felt cheated because "he never done got no education," so he hired the unemployed, fleeing refugee from Athens, Aristotle, to "learn" his little boy.

One of the high points in the life of Alexander the Great was that he was taught for a couple of years by this famed philosopher, Aristotle. This seems to have had as much of an effect on little Alexander as early Christian training had on Adolf Hitler. Aristotle, you will remember, is the great teacher who taught that the brain is an organ that exists merely for the purpose of cooling the blood and is not involved in the thinking process. This is only true of certain persons, says Willy Cuppy.

Alexander's mom, Olympias, was a cutesy herself. She liked snakes, and had them roaming all over the castle. And as Willy Cuppy says; "Having real snakes at home does an alcoholic no good, it just complicates matters." She had her husband assassinated, and then boiled one of his several other wives, alive.

To complicate Alexander's rise to "Greatness" coming from this background of dysfunctional family life, he was also burdened with a "sexual identity" problem. But being a Greek in those good-old-days, no one noticed.

He got drunk one evening and killed one of his best friends. This made him cry - the next day of course. He was too drunk the day he actually performed the dirty deed to cry, or laugh for that matter. He also crucified, Glaucias, the physician of Hephaestion, his roommate and lifelong companion.

Hephaestion died possibly of typhoid fever. Glaucias, obviously, had no malpractice insurance.

Alexander the Great was a real sweetheart. One can only marvel at anyone calling this man Great. How about Alexander the Terrible or Alexander the Lunatic, or Alexander the Sick and Deranged. Both he and his roommate died of fever and drunkenness. Lucky for all of us, he died at thirty-three. I should think that Alexander was the kind of kid who could have changed the Pope's mind on the value of abortion.

But let's not leave Alexander the Moron on a negative note. For some mystical reason he didn't persecute the Jews and was responsible for introducing the eggplant to Europe. What I guy!

Prescott Bush (1895-1972)

"... One of the partners of the Union Banking Corporation, the man who oversaw all investments on behalf of the Nazi-affiliated owners, happened to be Prescott Bush, grandfather of the American president George W. Bush. Through the connections of his father-in-law, Bert Walker (George W's maternal great-grandfather) who has been described by the U.S. Justice Department investigator as 'one of Hitler's most powerful financial supporters in the United States,' Prescott Bush specialized in managing the investments of a number of German companies, many with extensive Nazi ties." So says Max Wallace on pp 349-350 of his book *The American Axis*.

Being raised in Massachusetts, I remember that when John F. Kennedy ran for president, JFK's European diary was on sale everywhere. He had mentioned Adolf Hitler in a positive paragraph. His father Joe Kennedy was accused of almost anything and everything – a Nazi included – with little or no corroboration.

Prescott managed investments for a number of German companies many of which were tied up with Nazis. It is true that many Americans were tied up with Germany and the Nazis right up to 1941 and Pearl Harbor. But Prescott Bush appears to be the only one to have the assets of companies that he managed seized by the United States government under the Trading with the Enemy Act. These companies include: the Union Banking Corporation, the Hamburg-Amerika Line, the Holland-American Trading Corporation, the Seamless Steel Equipment Corporation and the Silessian-American Corporation.

Not that business as usual with the Nazis during World War II was uncommon. I.F. Stone gives a blow by blow description of this questionable behavior in his book, *The War Years 1939-1945,* and Charles Higham in his book *Trading with the Enemy,* provides a more historical account. I list only these two books but there are many others.

John Loftus, a former Justice Department Nazi war crimes investigator, and recent president of the Florida Holocaust Museum states in his book, *the War Against the Jews*, "The

69

Bush family fortune that helped put two family members in the White House can be traced directly to the Third Reich."

Loftus is not kind to Prescott Bush in his book. Loftus is equally unkind to Allan Dulles and his brother John Foster Dulles. Others like the infamous Kitty Kelley in her book, *The Family,* give Prescott a pass saying that he stopped dealing with the Nazis after Pearl Harbor. Loftus and others disagree. The fact that Prescott Bush's many companies' assets were seized is also suspicious. I don't know of any other company that had their assets seized. Loftus also suggests that Prescott avoids prosecution by volunteering to spy for the OSS. And strangely enough in 1951 assets of 1.5 million were returned to the Bush family. I guess it was all a case of mistaken identity.

William Jefferson Clinton (1946-)

President from 1993-2001

Bill Clinton has the unique distinction of being the first president ever in the history of the United States to be younger than me. God, I hate that! I am of the generation who vowed never to trust anybody over thirty. Now I don't trust anyone who is not over sixty-five. He is also the first Democratic president since F.D.R. to be elected for a second term. Clinton was definitely not one of our ex-war hero/general presidents.

Bill Clinton may also be the first president to have oral sex in the oval office (and possibly the Red Room, Blue Room, and Green Room) and while still engaged in conversation on the telephone, we are told. He was obviously not the first president to look the American people in the eye and lie. Lying is really a very old presidential political tradition.

Andrew Johnson is the only other president to undergo an impeachment proceeding. He was also impeached but not put out of office. He was also a Democrat who was being challenged by rightwing extremists.

Clinton's childhood background leads me to only one conclusion - Clinton was poor, white, southern, trailer trash. His mother was married to a traveling salesman who turned out to be a bigamist. His stepfather owned a used car lot, drank excessively and beat his wife. Bill, it seems, had to physically protect his mother on occasions. His mother went to school nights and eventually became a nurse.

Andrew Johnson and Andrew Jackson both come immediately to mind when contemplating Bill Clinton. All three of these presidents had very strong rightwing opposition. All three stood up to the challenge and all three were "good ole boys" from the South.

Jackson was as tough as nails, but common folk loved and admired him. Johnson was also as tough as nails but he was not so loved or admired. He had a real hard go, but eventually was re-elected to the Senate and was welcomed back to the

71

floor with flowers and cheers from his fellow Senators and the gallery.

For Bill Clinton and his Mrs., we all know, to the distress of many, that it ain't over, 'till it's over. Mrs. Clinton has already returned to Washington as a Senator and now as Secretary of State. And Bill, "America's first Black president," as I heard him referred to on TV by a black man at a black political forum, has opened some kind of political office in Harlem. Yes, HARLEM. To tell the truth, I don't really believe that Bill Clinton is black. I'm for an investigation.

Catherine the Great (1729-1796)

Now Catherine was really, really GREAT! If you don't believe me you can ask; Sergei Saltykov, Gregory Orlov and his brothers Ivan, Theodore, and Vladimir, Gregory Potemkin, Peter Zavadovsky, Lieutenant Zoritch, Korsakov, Lanskoy, Yermolov, Mamonov, Platon Zubov, Strahov, Levachov, Miloradovitch, Miklachevski and by some claims a minimum of three hundred others.

These supposed affairs cost the Russian government 92,820,000 rubles. Yeah but, were the Russians on a gold or silver standard at that time? It could have been all paper rubles and she had the printing press. So what's the real harm?

There were those who said that Catherine the Great was a whore. They say this just because she set up a private suite for her lovers right in the palace and paid them in advance to sleep with her.

Well, number one, she didn't sleep with just anybody. She always had two of her girl friends try them out first. Yes, she had a number of affairs but some of them were very, very short - a month, a week, some barely a night or two. And she never had them at the same time, always one after another. Even so, some accuse her of having slept with everybody. But, as my friend Willy Cuppy says, it never occurs to some of these critics that there were millions of men in Russia who Catherine never even met. And besides, whoever heard of a whore paying people to sleep with her. It's the other way around, ain't it? Besides, her husband was an imbecile. Well, technically he wasn't an imbecile, but everyone who knew him thought that he was, and that included his own mother. He liked to play with dolls, not real ones though, we can safely presume.

Strangely enough Catherine wasn't even Russian, she was German. Some say that she was the illegitimate daughter of Frederick the Great - nobody who really knows anything about Frederick the Great, though.

After a number of years of trying, Catherine finally gave up on Peter the imbecile and had the poor man put to sleep. After that, she decided to help the poor peasants. She quickly found out that the poor didn't really understand the nature of paper money either. They kept blaming her and all of her crazy spending and rich friends for all of their poverty. She gave out books on economics written by William F. Buckley and Newt Gingrich but they still didn't believe her. So she did her best to wipe most of them out and started a war or two to keep them all busy and off the streets.

She was an enlightened Tzarina and knew Voltaire, and the Encyclopedists. Denis Diderot (and possibly a few others) spent an evening or two at the palace. Catherine was really quite a girl, and she kept it up till the very end when she finally kicked the bucket at sixty-seven.

She had a bunch of kids, quite understandably. She even had a Russian word invented in her honor, Vremienchik - man of the moment. Some famous historians say, though she may have had many lovers, she never learned the real meaning of love. Yeah but, she sure gave it one heck of a try, and I for one give her a lot of credit for the attempt. She may never have learned the "real" meaning of the word love, but I'll bet she made up a lot of her own personal definitions that were darn close, even if she didn't succeed in getting them into some encyclopedia.

Constantine (280-337)

One of the most intriguing events in history is the rise and eventual establishment of Christianity. Why is that so intriguing?

Well basically because Christianity was not the religion of the dominant classes. Christianity was not the religion of the rulers but the ruled; not of the majority but the minority. Following the line of Christianity does not lead us back to the Egyptians, or the Romans or the Greeks, but to a laborer's son - the son of a carpenter, not the son of a king.

For some confusing reason it is Constantine, who gave us this flip-flop in what we should expect from human history.

For nearly three hundred years after the death of Christ the Roman rulers killed, murdered, and fed Christians to the lions. Then Constantine stopped feeding Christians to the lions and started feedings his lions Jews and hordes of other unfortunate non-believers. Why?

Christians say that it was a miracle of God, but one religion's miracle seems to mean another religion's evisceration. I would tend to doubt that God would stoop to take a side in the human propensity to slaughter one another over rather trivial differences of opinion.

It seems that a more practical explanation of the miracle of Constantine's conversion was the composition of the army he inherited from his dad. Constantine's dad was a powerful general. His mother was a serving wench in her dad's barroom in Drepanum. There remains the controversy of Constantine's legitimacy. But nobody is perfect, and you know how soldiers are.

Somehow Christians suddenly composed sixty percent of Constantine's army, while at the same time only comprising twenty percent of the Holy Roman Empire. What is more interesting is how a group of Christians who, according to Gibbon and others, wouldn't pay taxes, wouldn't take up arms in defense of their homelands, professed a communistic all-for-one, and one-for-all attitude when it came to material goods, and probably wouldn't salute the flag either, became soldiers. In fact, Christians wouldn't even say "may Jupiter bless you" after someone sneezed.

Constantine also had this thing about virginity. Any young man who seduced any young lady under the age of twenty-five was fed to the lions. And if the young lady admitted that the event was consensual, she was also fed to the lions. If a servant or slave assisted in this rape, he or she was forced to drink a cup of molten lead. Wow, molten lead! That sounds like a drink with a real bite too it.

Constantine, what was his story - I mean the real story?

Edward VIII
and Mrs. Simpson

King abdicates throne for "love."

What a wonderful story, huh? It could have been written by Eric Segal and produced and directed by little "Oppie" of the Andy Griffith show. The stars should have been Grace Kelly and Cary Grant. Ah yes, how sublime. But reality turns out to be quite different. Not only doesn't Mrs. Simpson resemble Grace Kelly in appearance or character, the real story could have been written by Stephen King or Robert Ludlum.

You can find a pretty good outline of the other side of this story in *Hitler and His Secret Partners*, written by James Pool or a biography of the colorful couple written by Charles Higham. It is quite a story.

The King of England turns out to be pretty much a Nazi; his mother, after all, was of German royalty.

Whatever attractive force Mrs. Simpson had, as my mother-in-law used to say, certainly didn't show. I've looked at every picture of Mrs. Simpson that I could find, and as far as I can determine, I'm sure that she shaved at least twice a day. Man, she is one rough looking female! But what she lacked in exterior beauty she made up for in her studies of the Karma Sutra and her meandering in Chinese brothels. It is not only pointed out that she spent some time in Oriental brothels but that she may have been employed in a couple of them. She was a well known playmate for the upper crust. One of her chums was the future son-in-law of Mussolini. We can only assume that the King's interest in Mrs. Simpson wasn't platonic.

It also doesn't hold up historically that the King abdicated for love. He had his royal butt booted out of the Palace by Stanley Baldwin, Winston Churchill and some of the other boys from the British government. He couldn't keep his German sympathies to himself. Every time he brought home any top secret information from the parliament it turned out to be tomorrow's news in the Berliner Tageblatt.

Not only do we find that the King of England was a Nazi himself, and Mrs. Simpson a royal humper for the "Rodney" class, she ain't even nice to our little lord Edward Adolf VIII.

She abuses him in public everywhere they go, ridicules him, has numerous affairs with both men and women, and continually calls him a bonehead for giving up the Crown. When Eddy decided not to be King anymore, he also decided that Mrs. Simpson wouldn't be Queen. This was a much more serious offense in the mind of Mrs. Simpson, and a lot of other women just like her.

Frederick the Great (1740-1786)

Frederick the Great, otherwise known as the philosopher king was neither "great" nor a philosopher. To give you some idea of what kind of a guy Freddy was, about two hundred years later, Adolf Hitler idealized the man.

Freddy's father, Frederick William I, was a German Teddy Roosevelt. He believed in carrying a big stick, but instead of walking softly, he thought it better to hit people with it. He was prone to walking around the streets of his Austrian princedom and beating the poor and unemployed, or little old ladies who were selling apples but not doing their knitting. He also used his stick to beat up little Freddy.

Frederick the not so Great was an obstinate little child. Whatever daddy liked, he liked the opposite. Freddy consequently liked the arts, wrote poetry, spoke French, and played the flute. He also liked other little boys. As a young man, he tried to run off to England with two of them. His daddy caught the naughty little boys and put one in prison for treason, and had the other one beheaded in plain view of Freddy's bedroom window. This did not succeed in changing Freddy's sexual direction in life. It did stop him from bringing any of his new boyfriends home to meet Pops though.

Freddy wrote a book about how a good philosopher king should act. It was published by Voltaire in 1740 and entitled, *Antimachiavell*. Shortly thereafter, he began invading countries and killing people. Very Niccolo Machiavellian of him, I would suggest.

Freddy liked to invite famous people to come and live at his palace. Voltaire was a house guest for three years, which makes one wonder a little about Voltaire. Freddy finally accused Voltaire of stealing some silverware or candlesticks or something, and Voltaire had to scat for his life. In retrospect, Voltaire said that Freddy was a "likable whore."

Freddy liked to write and wrote thirty-eight volumes of something that nobody, but probably Adolf Hitler, has ever read.

Freddy was also a part of Adolf's Jewish inspiration. He liked to kill or exile the poor ones, but the wealthier ones were allowed to live - for a price. They could also go from town to town - as long as they didn't mind paying a toll at every street corner and getting beat up and robbed by the local German population. One son of a "prized" or protected Jewish family was allowed to take a bride - for a price of course. Any other sons were forced to abstain from marriage or leave Berlin. Frederick passed a Jewish ordinance – *the Revidiertes General Privilegium und Reglement vor die Judenshaft.* You don't have to be able to read German to get the idea of that law.

Tom Paine wrote in his "Rights of Man" that if the world could get rid of its Kings and Royal families, the world would at last be free from war. I always wondered where Tom got such a naive idea, but reading about Freddy and the rest of the Royal families is beginning to make it all clear. And even if it didn't stop war, it might have been a fun thing to do, just for the hell of it.

Hirohito (1901-1989)

Imagine that Hitler was not dead at the time of the surrender of Germany and the initiation of the occupation government. Imagine that he is allowed to remain at his Palace and send representatives to sign the surrender documents because the Allies chose not to humiliate the great man. Imagine further, that he is to be included into the framework of the new government, and a number of his head honchos and military generals are to be included in the new government. He will also be surrounded by the richest and most powerful families in Nazi Germany. His private funds, amounting to over five billion dollars, secreted in Swiss and Argentine bank accounts, will not be bothered, and he will be given a tax free stipend of 22,000 dollars per year for his cooperation from American taxpayers. He will not be forced to renounce his title of Fuhrer (God, in Hirohito's case) but will be given a new title of divinely inspired king of the new constitutional monarchy. And, it goes without saying, he will not be put under any embarrassment or trial for any alleged war crimes that he may have been responsible for during his reign of aggression and terror as Fuhrer (God) and commander and chief.

With Hirohito, the emperor of Japan, you do not have to imagine, for this is what happened.

Hirohito was trained as a child by General Nogi, a Samurai warrior and hero of the 1905 war with Russia, to learn leadership and the Art of War. He was the leader of his nation and responsible for such actions as the unprovoked invasion of China; the sneak attack on Pearl Harbor; the rape of Nanking; the experiments and tortures of Chinese and American prisoners of war by General Shiro Ishii operating near Harbin in Manchuria - the infamous laboratories of the 731 Corps; the Bataan Death March; and the slaughter of 250,000 Chinese civilians at Chekiang in mid August of 1942 in reprisal for the Jimmy Doolittle raid of April 18, 1942 - just to name a few.

No, Hirohito is not forced to commit suicide, or leap to his death from the top of the imperial palace. No, Herohito will live and go on to die as one of the richest men to have ever lived. His tax free stipend of 22,000 thousand dollars a year (his occupational government Social Security check) would grow in just ten years to over three hundred thousand, and his personal yearly income to between forty-five and fifty million dollars. Not bad for a guy who was responsible for leading 25 million of his own people to their death.

The Russians and Chinese must be asking themselves today why they chose to fight as allies of the United States when history has proved it a million times more profitable to be one of its defeated enemies. And may I offer a suggestion to whoever it might be that is intending to start World War III. Your first target should be 'neutral' Switzerland and other independent banking nations of the world. At least then, if there are any spoils of this war; if you happen to be the victor maybe you might get some. In any case, your main plan should be, attack the United States, fight as briefly as possible, and then surrender "unconditionally" - whatever that means.

Adolf Hitler (1889-1945)

Adolf Schicklgruber (Hitler's real name) was recently voted the century's number one man on an internet poll, I am told. His selection was ignored and replaced with Albert Einstein.

There is no doubt that he and the image of his doctrine cast a shadow over this entire century. I have just finished reading his autobiography (Mein Kampf) for the third time and it has left me with a good many new insights and observations.

The first thing that I found shocking was the number of times Adolf refers to God, the Savior, the Almighty, the Supreme Authority, and the Prince of Peace etc. Before reading his book, I had the tendency to think of Adolf as a Godless creature, an atheist possibly, but it is plain that Adolf did not look at himself as such. In fact, Adolf becomes much more understandable when viewed from the perspective of a religious zealot or preacher – Osama bin Laden style. He felt that he was inspired or chosen by a divine hand. It is clear from his writing that Adolf Hitler considered himself an inspirational, divinely inspired prophet.

He traced his Christian type heritage from the barbarous, genocidal line of misguided Christian murders and killers stemming from the likes of a good many medieval popes - St. Bernard, the murderous initiator of the Crusades, Constantine, and Charlemagne, both extravagant, international murders who killed and slaughtered in the name of God and under the sign of a cross.

Next most shocking to me was Adolf's interpretation of history.

Adolf unabashedly states that it matters very little from an historical perspective how many individuals a particular leader slaughters under his reign. Adolf claims that it is clear from reading history books that all that will be remembered, a hundred or a thousand years hence, is how many great works of architecture - pyramids, coliseums, libraries, highways, and technological achievements - they left behind. So kill, torture and murder all you want, but build and invent and all will be forgotten and forgiven.

This seems to me to be a glaring message to those interested in history today. In the historian's attempt to salvage some good out of the horror of the human past, he must not forget to report what really happened, and what an immoral, un-Godly horror it really was.

I think it would be interesting today for example to re-evaluate our presidents from the perspective of how many others were killed, murdered or sacrificed to war under their reign. From this perspective where would we find Abraham Lincoln, Harry Truman, Dwight Eisenhower, Richard Nixon, FDR, Ronald Reagan, Bill Clinton, George Washington, George H.W. Bush and George W. Bush? If we counted bodies only, George Washington, Bill Clinton and Dwight Eisenhower would be the winners of the above presidential survey. Abraham Lincoln, Franklin D. Roosevelt and Harry Truman would be pulling up the rear. Calvin Coolidge and Warren G. Harding would look like real winners.

Thomas Jefferson (1743-1826)

President 1801-1809

It took thirty-six ballots in the House of Representatives to get Thomas Jefferson over Aaron Burr in their tie vote for the presidency. Actually Burr wasn't even running for the presidency. He was a candidate for the vice presidency at the time. Thomas Jefferson was a Republican.

George Washington and John Adams were both Federalist. The Federalists were the conservatives of their day and the Republicans were the liberals.

Thomas Jefferson didn't believe in having a standing army; he felt that the Navy should be nothing more than a Coast Guard, and that the American people should protect their freedom and independence by way of a voluntary militia. A large standing military only led a nation to foreign wars, he thought. But no sooner did he get into office than he sent the Army and Navy to Tripoli to fight the Barbary Pirates.

The Barbary Pirates were the terrorists or gangsters of their day. They were getting protection money from governments all over the world. Pay the premium and your ships would not be harassed. It took until 1805 for Jefferson to subdue the Barbary Pirates. This was all accomplished without authorization from Congress.

His famous Louisiana Purchase was not entirely without controversy either. He had only been authorized two million dollars to buy the port of New Orleans and secure shipping rights along the Mississippi. But when he found out that Napoleon was willing to sell, in addition to New Orleans, half the western continent for just sixteen million he immediately agreed to the sale without even consulting Congress. He put it through Congress not as a request but as a done deal.

He repealed the Federalist's Alien and Sedition acts, and pardoned all those under conviction due to their enactment. To Jefferson's thinking the Federalists were despots and dictators who did not have faith in a democratic society. The Federalist, especially archrival Alexander Hamilton, called Jefferson everything under the sun. Jefferson was called, in the conservative press of the day; a drunkard, the father of numerous mulattos because he was having a well publicized affair with one of his slaves, and an atheist. His wife Martha was half-sister to Sally Hemmings, Jefferson's rumored concubine and household slave. Sally Hemmings and Martha were from the same father, John Wayles.

Jefferson's election will undoubtedly bring about a Civil War and initiate a reign in which murder, adultery, robbery, rape and incest will be openly taught and practiced, so it was said. Alexander Hamilton, who seemed to be hell on roller-skates in those days, was finally shot in a duel with Aaron Burr who was no mild mannered, compassionate figure himself. Burr actually tried to get a country of his own going. He was eventually captured and tried for treason. But the politics of the day being pretty much like the politics of today, Burr was freed by Federalist, and Jefferson adversary, Judge John Marshall.

Jefferson was also responsible for the Lewis and Clark expedition and the drafting of the Declaration of Independence. In his original draft he tried to get slavery abolished, and blamed it all on the British. He established an embargo on trade trying to avoid a war with England and France that nearly bankrupted everybody.

Jefferson was another one of our reluctant leaders. He fought for the job, but was more than happy to see his term finally come to an end.

Abraham Lincoln (1809-1865)

President 1861-1865

Abraham Lincoln may not be all that he is cracked up to be, according to Gore Vidal in his book *"The Second American Revolution and Other Essays."*

Nancy Hanks, Abraham's mother was illegitimate, and this is documented by Abraham himself, says Gore.

He was no shy, modest, warm, gentle person. "No great man is ever modest. It was his intellectual arrogance and unconscious assumption of superiority that men like Chase and Sumner could never forgive," says John Hay, Lincoln's secretary.

He was no little po-boy, rail-splitter from a log cabin in the backwoods. By the time he became president he was a thriving, well to do, ambitious, aggressive lawyer.

Lincoln was not a good Christian. In fact, he wrote a book, *Infidelity.* "Lincoln, in that production, attempted to show that the Bible was false: first on the grounds of reason, and, second, because it was self-contradictory; that Jesus was not the son of God any more than any man." Herndon, Lincoln's law partner, friend and biographer confirms this account in his biography of Lincoln.

Lincoln spoke of God in later speeches, according to Gore, because of political pressure, but even so, made no references to Jesus.

Lincoln's wife, Mary Todd, went mad, and they had three sons who all died prematurely. This may be due to the fact that Lincoln around 1835-1836 went to Beardstown and contracted syphilis. He got treatment for it by a Doctor Daniel Drake in Cincinnati. He may have infected his wife, Mary, with the disease and hence her madness and the death of his three boys. This, claims Gore, may also explain his terrible bouts with melancholy, depression and chastity.

In 1846, as a Congressman, he opposed the war with Mexico on the grounds that it was a nasty, aggressive business started by the United States to seize new territories from a weaker opponent. In a speech thirteen years before the Civil War he declared, "Any people anywhere being inclined and having the power have the right to rise up and shake off the existing government, and form a new one that suits them better." OOPS!

Old Abe wasn't even a friend of the Negro, according to Mr. Vidal. He didn't precipitate the war to free the slaves or to abolish slavery, but to save the Union. "If slavery is not wrong, then nothing is wrong,"... but ... "if I can save the Union without freeing any slaves, I will do that. If I can save the Union by freeing some and leaving others alone, I will do that."

Early in his administration he and his Republican buddies acquired land in Central America for the purpose of re-locating American blacks. I guess he didn't know about Liberia. OOPS, again.

Gore goes on to credit Lincoln with the creation of the American Nation State. In other words, Gore claims that Lincoln, with his war, destroyed the Union and created a Nation.

I think old Gore has got his history mixed up with his fiction here. Lincoln did not start the Civil War. The South started the Civil War when it attacked Fort Sumter. And Lincoln did not deny the South their "right" to secede from the Union. The South gave up that right when they signed onto the Constitution... *"No State shall enter into any Treaty, Alliance or Confederation ... enter any agreement or compact with another State or with a foreign power or engage in war."*

So much for legal and social contracts, I suppose?

As previously stated Abraham Lincoln did not start the Civil War. The Cotton South started the Civil War even before Abraham Lincoln was inaugurated. They had been threatening secession and rattling their sabers for over twenty years. The Atlanta Confederacy proclaimed:

"Whether ... Pennsylvania Avenue is paved ten fathoms deep in mangled bodies ... the South will never submit to ... the inauguration of Abraham Lincoln."

The South was so aggressive and adamant on this slavery issue, I actually wonder if they intended or had a plan for conquering the North. With their aggressive attitude, it does seem difficult to believe that if they had been the victorious party in this conflict that they would have allowed the North to go on harboring runaway slaves or continue in their free slave state status. Did they want independence, or domination?

Abe, though a member of the rightwing, abolitionist Republican Party was not about to abolish slavery anytime soon. He was in favor of a slow turnover of the policy, one that might take ten, even twenty years. As stated above, he talked of a colonization program for transplanting discontented black and freed slaves in South America. His initial emancipation proclamation outraged his Republican cohorts in 1863. It freed slaves only in those areas of the Confederacy still in rebellion, not in any Southern States already occupied by the Union army, nor in any loyal slave states. After much criticism he announced to strong critics, such as Horace Greeley and William Garrison, that his goal as president was not to abolish slavery but to preserve the Union.

Lincoln was a hands-on Commander and Chief. He fired McClellan and replaced him with Burnsides. Burnsides was replaced by Hooker, and Hooker by General George Meade.

At the battle of Gettysburg a defeated and escaping Lee was trapped by the flooding Potomac. But disregarding Lincoln's orders, Meade hesitated and Lee escaped. Lincoln blamed Meade for missing the opportunity of ending the war.

It wasn't until U.S. Grant came along that Lincoln found a man that he trusted. When the press went to Lincoln criticizing Grant on his unwillingness to provide information about the war or his plans, Abe told them not to feel bad because General Grant wouldn't tell him anything either. When they criticized Grant for drinking too much whiskey, Lincoln asked them to find out what brand General Grant drank so that he could send a case of it to his other Generals.

When John Wilkes Booth shot Abraham Lincoln, point blank in the back of the head at the Ford Theater, while the newly re-elected president and his wife and some friends were watching the comedy, *Our American Cousin*, Mr. Booth may have executed the best friend a defeated army could ever have had.

There were many in the North who were screaming for execution for Confederate generals and political leaders, firing squads or imprisonment for officers and lesser personages, military occupation of all the rebellious states and land reform and redistribution of all Southern plantations and wealth. Lincoln's attitude was saintly when looked at from the point of view that this group of Southern conspirators and "traitors" were responsible by their belligerent attitude for the death of 600,000 thousand of their fellow citizens and probably double that number in wounded and maimed. And all for a cause that is considered by almost everyone today to be, not only immoral but unjust and criminal to humankind – the buying, selling, torture, abuse and trading of human life. Some say, cutely, that the issue of the Civil War was not slavery but State's Rights. But the right that the Southern States were trying to secure was slavery. No matter how one attempts to spin it, the issue was slavery.

Richard Milhous Nixon (1913-1994)

President 1969-1974

John F. Kennedy assassinated. Martin Luther King assassinated. Bobby Kennedy assassinated. The ghettoes were a cinder. The college campuses were in a state of revolution. The streets of America were filled with burning American flags, protesters of one nature or another and people fist fighting in their living rooms.

I remember watching film clips of the 1968 Democratic Convention on TV. I couldn't believe that it was the United States of America. I thought it was some banana republic involved in another coup.

Richard Nixon was the Republican and Hubert Humphrey was the Democrat. Nixon couldn't speak and Humphrey wouldn't stop. But they both had pretty much the same story. They were going to end the war in Vietnam. Lyndon had quit the battle; no guts, said Harry Truman. But Humphrey had been Lyndon's vice president and right-hand man. Would he really end the war and reverse his old boss and the whole Democratic Party? Nixon was Eisenhower's vice president for eight years. Ike promised that he would end the war in Korea and he did. Could Tricky Dickey be of the same cloth?

Nixon cut his political teeth in the post F.D.R., communist bashing era. He won his seat in the Senate, bashing a Mary Cohagan Douglas. He called her a socialist and a commie. He was one of McCarthy's dirty dozen. He played big in the Alger Hiss case and the Pumpkin Papers. Tricky Dickey made a lot of enemies during this anti-commie period. He ruined a lot of lives and destroyed the careers of a slew of prominent hopefuls. He and McCarthy and comrades struck down big names. Those attacked, along with their children, friends and relatives came back to haunt Tricky Dickey. Nixon and crowd didn't pull any punches and weren't freighted of fabricating information or doctoring photos to make a point.

"I am not a crook," said Richard Nixon, and there are those today who claim that he never really did anything worse than other political leaders. I always thought that this claim of innocence on Nixon's part was nothing but hogwash until I started reading about the life and times of other of our presidents. But whatever, there is no doubt that Nixon liked to dabble on the edge of legal legitimacy. In one of his campaigns, he sent out a card which claimed to have been sponsored by conservatives in the Democratic Party. The card advertised the support and backing of these Democrats. He had no such support from any such group. But just to make matters worse, he had these supposed supporters also make a request for financial support on this card, giving HIS address as the proper place to send their contributions.

Was this illegal or just cleaver? Well a court decided that this definitely was illegal, and banned such type activity to future political aspirants. Nixon, as innovator of this technique, was excused from any prison time. Was THIS illegal - seems like an even better question. Because this exact crime had never been committed previously, Nixon should be let off the hook? I don't think so.

Nixon won his first term as president in a very close election with no opposition claims of foul play. But his landslide victory over McGovern in 1973 was not considered quite so evenhanded. If you were a McGovern supporter and donated money to the cause, you very quickly found yourself and/or your business being investigated by the I.R.S. Was this illegal?

Whatever you might think, this practice had long ago been declared illegal. But was there any proof that Nixon had actually authorized these I.R.S. incursions? Apparently not; so no prison time here either. In the midst of this second campaign we have new political borders being challenged - the Watergate scandal.

Four years had passed and Nixon hadn't fulfilled his promise of ending the war in Vietnam. A good many people were not very happy about this. One of these people was a man named Daniel Ellsberg. He had worked for the Department of Defense during the Johnson administration, and had access to information with regards to the war. He knew that the Federal Government was lying to the American people about the war under Johnson and now under Nixon. He decided to expose this to the public in what is now known as the *Pentagon Papers*.

Nixon had been working on stopping leaks in the White House. He had put on a staff of "plumbers." In the case of Ellsberg it was decided by the administration that he was a traitor to his country and was "undermining the war effort" by giving out secret information to the public and our enemies overseas. Nixon felt that he should be silenced, put in jail or at least discredited.

The "Plumbers & Associates" broke into Ellsberg's psychiatrist's office looking for information that could discredit Ellsberg personally. Maybe he was a psychopath, paranoid, or schizophrenic; or possibly something even worse, like a man who cheated on his wife or dressed funny on Wednesday nights.

From the psychiatrist's office, the Plumbers then went to the National Democratic Party headquarters at the Watergate Hotel. What they were looking for is the subject of much speculation, but whatever, the bozos got caught. Getting caught is one of the chief qualifications of becoming a criminal. If you never get caught, you can not legitimately claim to be one. Richard Nixon didn't do any of the breaking and entering, and, at the time, it couldn't really be proven that he had authorized any of this activity. So why was he threatened with impeachment and once threatened, did he resign?

Well, it seems that Richard Nixon was audio taping his presidency for prosperity. Other presidents had done the same thing. Knowledge of these tapes became known to the investigating committee, and it was discovered that Nixon knew about the illegal activities of his hired Plumbers and then proceeded to make attempts to cover up their exploits. Tricky Dickey was not ahead of his time on this one. This was already considered a crime, and now Tricky Dickey had been caught. So contrary to his claim, Richard Nixon was and is a crook. He broke the law and got caught doing it. So why didn't he go to prison?

This is really one of the most outstanding episodes in American presidential history. Richard Nixon's vice president, Spiro Agnew, had been formally charged with having accepted bribes as governor of Maryland and as Vice President. Ten years later Agnew paid the state of Maryland $270,000.

Richard Nixon at a later date was also found guilty of tax evasion, and was fined $300,000. Spiro Agnew was the first Vice President in U.S. History to be forced to resign due to criminal charges. Richard Nixon was the first President to be forced to resign for any reason.

Richard Nixon then appointed Gerald Ford, vice president, after which he conveniently resigned the presidency. Gerald Ford then promptly pardoned and absolved Nixon of his sins and any prison time that he might have had coming.

So there you go, a Russian classic novel, *Crime and No Punishment*. But nevertheless Richard Nixon must be awarded the prize of being America's first legitimately criminal president – even though he did no actual prison time – he did "plea bargain." Gerald Ford in his memoirs stated that he demanded that Nixon sign an admission of guilt before he would grant Nixon his pardon.

Peter the Great   (1672-1725)

Russian Emperor 1682-1725

If you consider Caligula and possibly Nero to be "Great," then I suppose you might consider Peter pretty "Great" too. It is almost guaranteed that people in history who have Great before or after their names, were not very Great at all. If you want to hear somebody say something Great about Peter, don't ask any Russians named Goldburg or Silverman. Don't ask his sister Sophia either. She tried to have him murdered and he locked her up in prison. Don't ask his first wife Eudoxia either. She got the room next to Sophia.

As a child he was "indulged" and very playful. It seems that he knocked somebody's teeth out with a pickax and blew somebody's head off with a homemade rocket. This and other precocious behavior, I guess, led him to become Tsar by the age of ten.

Peter decided to go abroad and find out how the real people lived. He went incognito and worked as a common laborer. It was hard to be incognito when you're six foot eight and a half, like to wear thigh high leather boots, and speak with a Russian accent as thick as a bowl of borscht.

He did just about as well as a laborer as he did at being incognito. He arrived at work two hours late, took three hours for lunch and left two hours early. His favorite beverage was vodka. When he returned from the West, possibly running out of vodka, he began putting what he had learned abroad into action at home.

He immediately started killing everybody. He started off by executing the Streltsi, the National Guard of Moscow. On the first day he chopped off two hundred heads, himself. When he got bored chopping off heads, he hung a few, roasted some others over a slow fire, and buried the rest alive. He displayed about two thousand of his beheaded victims for his public's delight by laying their bodies about the city all winter.

His second wife was named Marta, she was a peasant. He really liked her. By the time he decided to marry her and change her name to Catherine, she had already given birth to five of his children.

He had a son named Alexis whom he was not very impressed with. The look on the kid's face just made Peter want to punch him. One day he got a little carried away and he beat little Alexis to death. But as Willy Cuppy says, he only did it once, and he was drunk at the time.

After awhile even Marta (Catherine) got a little loose. She had an affair. Peter, jokester and good sport that he was, had the man decapitated, put his head in a bottle and had it placed in Marta's window.

In reforming Russia, Peter made everybody cut off their beards, including the women and children. Anyone who wanted to keep their beard could buy permission. But they had to wear a license plate proving that they had done so.

Peter was quite a guy and ahead of his times, as far as Russian Tsars go. He met the Archbishop of Canterbury in person and got an honorary degree of law from the University of Oxford. Besides, anybody who likes midgets and dwarfs can't be all bad.

Ronald Wilson Reagan (1911- 2004)

President - 1981-1988

Ronald Reagan's political career begins in the post F.D.R. era and the period called McCarthyism. Reagan, at the time, was the president of the Screen Actors Guild and a McCarthyite, like his buddy Richard M. Nixon. Reagan was one of those who went before the McCarthy Committee and ratted on his friends and associates. He, Humphrey Bogart and Jimmy Stewart, were all of the same political attitude. I don't really think that Bogart had the so called patriotic, anti-Communist motivation of Reagan and Stewart. Bogart was just cowardly. In honor of that position or characterization Bogart was cast in his next movie, *The Treasure of Sierra Madre*, to coincide with that public perception. He was a big success in duplicating the behavior of a coward.

It is suggested that Reagan may have lost his first wife over this political change of character. He was a Democratic. He went from Democrat to McCarthyite to Republican. Reagan claims to have "seen the light," but his turn from a defender of the poor and destitute to a heroic supporter of the rich and famous may have been somewhat influenced by his romance and eventual marriage to his second wife, the daughter of a multimillionaire.

Reagan came to redeem us from the Carter malaise, and in his first term as president, he did. Carter, in the campaign, had accused Reagan of being trigger happy. Reagan had, after all, been an advocate and defender of the Barry Goldwater candidacy. Reagan's eventual gunboat philosophy and ability to bomb anybody anywhere frightened the heck out of a lot of Democrats. But, it seemed to work. Of course, there are those that claim he planted the seeds to our current terrorist's problems, but it is easier to blame Clinton.

Reagan is another of our non-general/non-lawyer presidents. He was only a war hero in the movies. In real life, he was an actor and radio announcer. In his first day in office, the 444 day Iran Hostage Crisis ended. A dilemma that Carter couldn't seem to solve was ended in one day, seemingly by Ronald Reagan's presence alone. While Republicans roared with delight, Democrats sat in suspended contemplation, wonder, admiration and bewilderment. How had he done it? The answer seemed to come to many around the year 1986 in the form of the Iran Contra affair.

It was suddenly discovered, against all of Reagan's personal protestations that he was, in fact, playing Let's-Make-a-Deal with the radical Iranian government. Not only was he trading arms for hostages, which he promised that he never, ever would do, but he was involved in a whole array of other very suspicious activities.

These activities included: subverting the Congress who were not even informed or aware of these arms sales or of any monies earned from these sales; trading weapons illegally, via a Jewish Government intermediary, to hostile, hostage taking Iran; hiding the illegally gained profit in a Swiss bank; and smuggling drugs, and financing revolutionary guerrilla activities which had already been denied funding by Congress due to the inability to determine the good guys from the bad guys.

In *the Secret War against the Jews* by John Loftus and Mark Aarons the authors claim that George Herbert Walker Bush was the real mastermind of this operation and Reagan was once again napping.

Ronald Reagan then was brought before an investigating committee. Obviously suffering from Alzheimer's disease, it quickly became evident that he could barely remember anything. Ollie North who had originally been selected as the fall guy refused to fall and the ex-General Poindexter took the hit. Poindexter was convicted in 1990. His conviction was reversed in 1991 due to a technicality – another chapter for the great Russian novel *Crime and No Punishment*.

Ollie swore under oath that to his understanding the President of the United States, Ronald Reagan, was completely aware and approved his activities. In fact, he restated this in the very first pages of his memoir.

Reagan may have relieved our malaise but now as he turned to walk away we saw a mask of the face of Richard Nixon strapped to the back of his head. Unlike Nixon, he didn't try to cover up his misdeeds; he just couldn't remember any of them.

It seems interesting to me that with all of the misdeeds and illegal activity of the Iran Contra Affair, the only thing that the investigating committee was interested in was whether or not the president had authorized or was aware of the diversion of the illegal funds that had been gained from the transaction and deposited in a Swiss bank account. It didn't matter that he had lied to all of the American people about a very, very important point of American policy - refusing to trade arms for hostages. It didn't matter that he may have lied, subverted, or somehow misled the entire United States Congress by selling Government property (missiles, rockets and the like) without their knowledge and or permission. I hate to be so blunt, but in real life this would be called stealing, robbery, embezzlement, something! Taking something that doesn't belong to you and then selling it to somebody else and then keeping the money in a Swiss bank account?

To determine that such behavior is against the law does not take a political scientist, or a Harvard law school expert. And then the fact that a group of men who were supposedly authorized by him personally or his close representatives in the Government, C.I.A. director Casey, and others, to smuggle drugs, sell them for a profit and use the money to buy weapons for the political overthrow of a neutral government; thus, supporting a group who had already been determined unworthy by the United States Congress, also has to be considered somewhat criminal, I should think.

Then we must also wonder - if Ronald Reagan could authorize all of that with a clear conscience, could it also be possible that all of this dirty dealing had actually started way back in campaign number one?

Is anyone now investigating the possible treasonous behavior of Mr. Reagan cutting an arms for hostages deal while competing with the then incumbent Jimmy Carter?

I mean, come on, the very day of his inauguration they release the hostages? In light of what we now know about the Reagan administration, this must loom as a very and highly probable possibility.

Now I do agree that it is too late to have Ronald Reagan executed like the Rosenbergs, or put in jail for life in light of his Alzheimer's condition and the fact that he is now deceased. And really there was no declared war with Iran at the time, but then there was no war with Russia at the time of the Rosenbergs or Alger Hiss and others who we convicted and punished in the past. In the case of Hiss, he was punished for much less egregious behavior. In the case of the Rosenbergs, they were put to death for transferring information that Harry Truman offered to share with the Russians a few years earlier. The Russians declined the offer. They already knew how to make an atomic bomb.

Ronald Reagan, it does seem very likely as a private citizen, cut a deal with a country that had for all extent and purposes declared war with us by taking our embassy and its representatives hostage - a flagrant violation of international law.

If Jane Fonda is labeled a traitor for giving succor and comfort to an enemy by sitting on a tank, what do we call a person who steals a tank from the U.S. Government then sells the tank to an enemy, along with a few missiles and other military hardware? A patriot? I think not. A Politician seems to be as accurate as we can get, I suppose. And may I paraphrase a famous Republican hero and say: Extremism in the name of undermining American government and American principles and ideals is not patriotism.

A few other things that we can thank Mr. Reagan for are:

A national debt greater than the accumulated debt of all of the other presidents who came before him, combined - a debt that for the first time in history grew at an even faster rate than the U.S. economy (and inflation) could compensate for. It was during Mr. Reagan's administration that most terrorists the world is now attempting to subdue were bought, supplied, or financed - this includes Osama bin Laden, the Contras, Saddam Hussein, the Taliban and probably any others that we may be hearing about in the years to come.

Reagan will also be remembered as the biggest modern day union buster since his name sake Woodrow Wilson and his personal hero Calvin Coolidge. Ronnie made firing people and cutting worker's wages heroic instead of a disgrace. He also killed the Public Higher Education idea for good. No longer do Americans look forward to the day that their child, if qualified, will be able to go to college for free. Instead they can look forward to paying off a debt greater than their poor parents ever imagined.

Ronnie encouraged his business friends to take American jobs overseas and with the help of a few of his friends gave them the scam of "cooking" the books. It was Ronnie's spending that brought us both the saving and loan and the commercial banking collapses - this is a fiasco that we have still not seen the end of and was the biggest payoff from the people (taxpayers) to a capitalist business enterprise in all of American History to that date

But most of all we can thank Ronald Reagan for reviving the spirit and practice of war here in the United States and around the world. Ronnie set the groundwork with Granada and Tripoli, which gave his assistant (Bush 41) the courage to attack Panama followed by Desert Storm. Now Junior has brought us full circle to Vietnam (Iraq) all over again; this has all served to achieve the main objective of re-establishing an international arms race that will certainly please his old Death Valley boss GE and others. Soon all the world will be buying or seeking the where-with-all to start their own nuclear projects. We are probably looking forward to the greatest arms race in all of history. But what should we have expected from the spokesman and loyal employee of one of the greatest arms producers in the world. Oh and by the way, the first thing Ronnie did when he got into office was give General Electric the greatest tax break in the history of the Company. By the time Ronnie was done, GE went from paying hundreds of millions in taxes to having the United States government owing them money - they actually got a credit.

Ronnie may have been loyal to his wife and his ex-employer but in my opinion he was a traitor to his class, to his roots and ancestry, to the workingmen of America and to the American system of government.

Theodore Roosevelt (1858-1919)

President from 1901-1909

I suppose that it would sound bigoted of me, if I were to say that Teddy was a little, rich boy, but Teddy WAS a little, rich boy. And, it seems, like all little, rich boys, he was in search of an achievement. It is claimed that Teddy was very bright and had a photographic memory - which is very advantageous depending on what it is that you chose to photograph with your photographic memory.

Teddy went to Harvard. His dad was a Republican who supported Abraham Lincoln during the Civil War, but his mother - Martha "Mittie" Bulloch - was a southern belle who often complained of the inconveniences brought to her by the loss of her personal slaves. She had two brothers who served in the Confederate Navy and she sent food and clothing, via agents in New York, to support the Confederate cause.

When his dad died Teddy inherited $125,000 from his estate. And when his mother died on February 14, 1884, Teddy inherited another $62,500. On the same day and in the same house, Teddy's first wife - Alice Hathaway Lee died from Bright's disease. She was only 22 years old. Apparently these inheritances were considered substantial in those days.

Not long after Mittie's passing Teddy married a good friend of his younger sister and an early childhood sweetheart of his. Her name was Edith Kermit Carow and she was the daughter of a prominent merchant.

Teddy was a third cousin twice removed of president Martin Van Buren, a fifth cousin of Franklin D. Roosevelt, and uncle of Eleanor Roosevelt, and a great uncle of Joseph Alsop and Stewart Alsop, both well known journalists of their time.

Teddy's daughter Alice married in the East Room of the White House. She lived to the age of 96 and was considered by society folks to be Washington's other monument.

Ethel, Teddy's other daughter married a Doctor and during WWI she served as a nurse to her husband in the American Ambulance Hospital in Paris.

Teddy oldest boy, Teddy Jr., became a soldier and eventually a Brigadier General. He received a Purple Heart, the U.S. Distinguished Service medal and eventually in WWII, the Congressional Medal of Honor. He served as Assistant Secretary of the Navy under President Harding; he was appointed governor of Puerto Rico and then governor-general of the Philippines by Coolidge; and he ran for Governor of New York against Al Smith but lost.

Kermit, Teddy's second son was also a soldier. He ended up dying of natural causes while on duty in the U.S. Army in Alaska.

Archibald was also a soldier. He was severely wounded in WWI and discharged as disabled. He joined up again and was severely wounded once again. And he was again discharged as disabled.

Quentin became an Army Air Corps pilot and was shot down and killed by German fighter planes during WWI.

Teddy, himself, served as a member of the New York National Guard. He commanded the U.S. Volunteer Cavalry Regiment, known as The Rough Riders and is famous for charging up Kettle Hill, in the San Juan Hills in Cuba.

As a child, little Teddy was rather sickly suffering from asthma. Teddy was so sickly he had to be tutored at home. When he wasn't sick or bedridden he was hyperactive and mischievous. He was kind of a nerd. He liked bugs and held aspirations of becoming a zoologist. Being small, nerdy, and needing glasses other kids had a tendency to beat him up. His dad bought him a gym and Teddy became a physical fitness fanatic and a boxing expert.

Teddy was somewhat religious but didn't really seem to favor any one particular religion over another. He attended the Dutch Reformed, Presbyterian, Episcopal, Grace Reformed, Christ Church etc. He didn't care much for many of the teachings of Lutherans or Calvinists or even Roman Catholics.

With all this religion he was nevertheless a firm believer in the separation of Church and State. He campaigned against the idea and practice of stamping "In God We Trust" on U.S. coins. His reasoning was interesting. He felt that stamping the name of God on money was insulting to God. He considered it sacrilegious.

Teddy was obviously one of those wealthy people who didn't necessarily believe that his wealth was a direct inheritance from God and therefore worthy of worshipping. He chose to worship God directly and not money or those who thought they possessed it at God's discretion. This is one of the reasons that many wealthy people considered Teddy a traitor to his class.

At first Teddy thought he would pursue law, but then on second thought, he felt more could be attained if he were to become one of the "ruling class." So he got into politics and the New York political machine.

Unfortunately, as mentioned above, Teddy was somewhat of a problem and an embarrassment to his class. He kept trying to reform everything. He kept calling rich people criminals and making reference to the "tyranny of wealth" but then the war with Spain came along, and Teddy was thrilled. He ordered a uniform appropriate from Brooks Brothers, and was off to San Juan Hill (Kettle Hill) with his own personal army of Rough Riders. Some historian's praise his effort as a heroic action while others claim it to be a rather foolhardy and misguided endeavor of unnecessary gallantry. George Seldes in his book *Witness to a Century* states, "Edward Marshall who operated his newspaper syndicate out of the offices of the Chicago Tribune ... was an admirer of Theodore Roosevelt; nevertheless he was an honest enough journalist to tell us that the famous 'charge up San Juan Hill' which eventually put T.R. in the White House, never took place. Marshall told me: Theodore Roosevelt did not 'charge' up San Juan Hill. Nobody 'charged'. How can you charge if you have no horses? Our regiment of cavalry had no horses at that time. The horses were still on the mainland, in Florida. We walked. It is true there was still some firing.

"Do you know who greeted Roosevelt when we reached the top of San Juan Hill – walking? A company of Negro cavalrymen – dismounted of course. They had got there first. But no one ever gave Negroes any credit in those days."

In any case, Teddy got his picture in the papers and then before you knew it, he was Governor of New York.

He liked being Governor of New York, but the New York political machine bosses did not like Teddy. Senator Thomas Platt, one of the big boys, was pretty upset with little Teddy. He is quoted as saying; "I want to get rid of the bastard. I don't want him raising hell in my state any longer." Teddy continued talking about things like the tyranny of wealth and the criminal rich. So the big boys in New York thought that the best thing for Teddy, the very popular war hero and man of the people, would be a nice safe place under a rock somewhere.

They couldn't find a big enough rock, so what greater position of obscurity and anonymity in government could there be than the Vice Presidency. So they got him drafted and then nominated as Vice President under their stalwart friend of big business and champion of the rich and powerful, Mr. McKinley.

McKinley was not very happy with the choice and Mark Hanna, McKinley's finance and campaign manager, warned the big boys that there was now only one life between the White House and a mad man.

After McKinley's assassination, Hanna cried; "Now look, that damn cowboy is President of the United States."

Once President, Teddy was hard to get rid of - everybody liked him. He kept badmouthing and harassing the big money boys. He became the friend of "Teddy Bear" cubs and tree huggers and did his best to make enemies of the railroads, and the giant trusts – at least publicly. But whatever he was doing, he was doing it right because Morgan, Harriman, Rockefeller, Frick and Gould backed him for a second term.

He put thousands of acres aside for National Parks and monuments; sent the U.S. Navy around the world; bought the first airplane from the Wright brothers to start the U. S. Air Force; dug the Panama Canal - which he claimed to have stolen fair and square; he invited a Negro to eat at the White House, Booker T. Washington; and negotiating a treaty between the Russians and the Japanese (Russo-Japanese War 1904-5) won him the Nobel Peace Prize. He was not exactly thrilled receiving the Nobel Peace Prize and he did let it be known that he thought that war was good and proper - it built character.

Teddy did think that war should be periodically interrupted by short intervals of peace. I would suppose he thought that to be necessary to give the nations of the world time to re-arm.

Once Teddy got rolling there was no stopping him. After losing the Republican nomination to Taft, but feeling as fit as a "bull moose" he ran for President, nominated by the Progressive Party.

While he was about to give a speech in Milwaukee a would-be assassin ran up to him and put a bullet into his chest. The bullet went through his written speech which he had in his pocket; then through his metal eyeglass case; and then sunk four inches into his chest. He coughed into his hand to see if there was blood in his lung, and then went on to speak before the crowd for fifty minutes. He didn't win. He split the Republican ticket, stopped Taft from getting a second term, and got a Democrat, Woodrow Wilson, elected.

Teddy was also an author. He wrote numerous history and true life adventure books. He wrote many newspaper and magazine articles and was quite a popular and interesting writer in his time.

Teddy was as you might have expected active up until the very last moments of his exciting and involved life. His active and daring life may have contributed to his somewhat early demise in 1919 at age sixty-one. He suffered from recurrences of malaria and a leg infection gained roaming with his boy Kermit in the jungles of Brazil.

He was writing and criticizing President Wilson the very day before he died. His last words were not very prophetic, exciting or philosophical. He told his valet James Amos to "please turn out the light" as he left his bedroom. Teddy died quietly and peacefully in his sleep.

Roosevelt, Franklin Delano (1882-1945)

President from 1933-1945

In 1924 Roosevelt (Rose-velt) went to the Democratic convention to place Alfred E. Smith's name before the gathering for nomination as Democratic presidential candidate. About three years earlier Roosevelt had been struck down with infantile paralysis (polio). The doctors thought that he would never walk again. They had doubts as to whether or not he would even sit-up again. But in less than three years, there he was at the Democratic National Convention struggling to the podium on crutches and harnessed in metal leg braces. It was only ten steps, but it seemed to take forever as the auditorium hushed and watched the poor man struggling to the microphone. When he got there he threw his head back and beamed his famous grin and the audience roared with a standing ovation that lasted an hour and thirty minutes.

On February 15, 1933, one month before his inauguration, a man named Giuseppe Zangara, sprayed the platform at Bayfront Park in Miami, with gunfire, wounding five of the president's entourage and killing Mayor Anton Cermak of Chicago.

Roosevelt came in with a bang. He won the popular vote by over seven million and the electoral vote 472 to 59 - not only that, but the Democrats swept the house and the Senate. They now controlled two thirds of the Senate and three quarters of the house. Why?

The U.S. government, the capitalist system, and all of its institutions were in the state of collapse. The American monetary system failed. The banking system failed. The Stock Market failed. Agriculture failed. Industry failed. The educational system failed. Labor and management were at war. Housing failed. Medical and hospitalization failed. No matter where one looked on the horizon, one saw chaos, collapse and corruption.

Whether this is all a part of a super-wealth conspiracy to bankrupt the middle class and thus control them, the poor, and the rebellious working class; or the built-in inevitability of an unrestricted competitive system; or just the workings of fate, the people of the United States were desperate.

Since Hoover took over the reigns of state everything had degenerated and the Republicans seemed to have no answer.

They weren't in favor of reform, relief, or revolution. Their only answers were poverty, police and Providence. The Republican Party had been in a state of known and visible corruption since the days of Ulysses S. Grant.

Hoover said that grass would be growing in the streets of America if Roosevelt was elected. By the time Hoover was finished the grass was already there, it only remained for Roosevelt to hire some of Hoover's fifteen million unemployed and starving to mow it. Roosevelt did much more than that. In just eight years he had half of that fifteen million back to work, and most of America smiling and beaming with hope and optimism once again.

He was called a traitor to his wealthy, privileged class. Hoover called him a Red and a Communist. The more reserved Republicans called him a socialist and a dictator. Joe Kennedy called him "that crippled son of a bitch that killed my son, Joe."

The man in the street who suddenly found himself once again with a job, food on the table for his family, a roof over his head and hope for the future, called him a savior from God Almighty. And these people elected him four times for a period of almost sixteen years. If he had not died, they would have probably elected him again.

Roosevelt not only had the hearts and minds of the people but the Congress and Senate also. He was given the powers of a president at war and for the first four years they passed just about everything that he proposed.

Roosevelt had promised to try anything and if it didn't work, try something else.

Hoover didn't leave the vault as low as Benjamin Harrison had left it for Grover Cleveland, but he did his best to leave Roosevelt with as little as possible. In the four months between Hoover's loss at the polls and Roosevelt's inauguration, Hoover and his buddies did their best to leave Roosevelt without a dime to work with.

The first thing Roosevelt did was to take hold of the money supply. He took the nation off the gold standard which had Europe screaming foul. He stopped all gold from leaving the country and pulled all gold certificates from circulation. He made owning gold illegal. He reduced the gold reserve backing on the American paper by nearly fifty percent, thus enabling him to double the amount of paper money in circulation.

The rich were now taking all of their money out of circulation and hiding it, or investing it in more prosperous foreign countries like fascist Italy and Nazi Germany. If that Communist, Socialist, Dictator Roosevelt was going to take up the side of those lazy, poor, good-for-nothings who were trying to ruin this country, he wasn't going to do it with their money.

Roosevelt did everything he knew to increase the revenue of the Federal Government. He cut government salaries and wages, and then spent it as fast as he could on programs to put people to work or relieve those without work opportunities. By 1938 he had put all of the 15 million unemployed to work temporarily and half of them permanently.

He set up federal mortgage and loan companies that basically bought up mortgages and loans from the banks and returned them to the borrowers at rates of payment that they could afford. He did the same for small businessmen and farmers, plus guaranteed the sale prices of farm commodities. The government even bought the farmer's surplus and gave the excess pork, butter, and bread etc., to the unemployed.

He got the banks straight and guaranteed deposits up to five thousand dollars. He subsidized medical care and tried to establish federal healthcare insurance. He plugged the holes in the Stock Market with a Securities and Exchange Commission that guaranteed a stock's legitimacy. He put Joe Kennedy in charge of the operation. When critics asked him why he put the biggest thief the business world and the Stock Market ever knew in charge of the whole deal - the big bad wolf right inside the chicken coop - he laughed and told them that it takes a thief to catch a thief.

He passed a National Industrial Recovery Act which set up public works projects, fair trade practices among business, and gave workers the right to strike and demand that bosses arbitrate grievances. Prior to this, strikes by workers were considered illegal and troops were sent in to break strikes and punish workers.

He opened up trade relations with Russia by recognizing the Soviet Union, the existence of which had been denied by the U.S. since 1917. This put fire to the notion that America really had a communist in the White House.

He set up an emergency housing division that cleared slums and built public and private homes.

He tried to build up the Navy and the Air Force by proposing the Vinson Naval Parity Act but congress refused to appropriate the money. The country was so much against war or our entry into a war that in 1938 they tried to pass the Ludlow Resolution. This resolution would not only deny the executive, but the Congress the right to declare war without a national referendum except in case of invasion.

He passed a tax - charging millionaires up to 75% on every million after their first.

He started a Federal Arts Project, a Federal Theater Project, a National Youth Employment Project; he even commissioned history and science research and a writer's project. He regulated the health and sanitation of food, meats, and drugs.

He started building dam and river projects in Tennessee, Colorado and in Michigan; and in 1936 even the beleaguered Bonus Army that Hoover had beat-up got the adjusted Compensation Act passed over F.D.R.'s veto. Over $1,500,000,000 in benefits were paid out to over three million veterans.

It seemed that up until this period in time the country was allowed to progress without rhyme or reason or rule and regulation. There had been no referee, no judge of fair play, and nobody who cared or who could do anything about it. Roosevelt came and America had its Moses, the law giver. He had a law, a plan or a program for everything.

In his first eight years his only opposition seemed to be the Supreme Court. They had been placed in their positions before he got control. They tried their best to declare unconstitutional everything that he attempted. But as fast as they declared it unconstitutional, the legislature passed a different but similar law to replace it.

By 1938, the rightwing Republicans had finally gotten together with the Klu Klux Klan Democrats from Dixie and the

110

tide began to turn. In the 1936 presidential election Roosevelt won by the largest electoral victory in a contested race in history ... 503 to 8. Even though 80% of the nation's newspapers came out for and supported Governor Landon, Roosevelt won the popular vote by over eleven million. But with the mid-term elections of 1938 the Republicans recovered 81 seats in the house and 8 in the Senate. They cut spending and put the depression back in business.

War was coming.

Now Roosevelt had to take on Hirohito, Mussolini and Adolf Hitler. Most of the free people of the world were in the clutches of dictators. Democracy was on its knees. Roosevelt as commander and chief would now have to win World War II while sick and from a wheelchair.

George Washington (1732-1799)

President from 1789-1796

George Washington, well, well ... no wooden teeth, no cherry tree, and it is even questionable whether he won the American Revolution or not. If it weren't for the French joining in at Yorktown, doubling the size of George's army and providing a navy offshore, Cornwallis probably would never have surrendered.

George may also have been sterile or impotent. His pear shape and particular ailments may have been indicative of a genetic distortion precipitous of this condition. This may explain his marriage to Martha - no children of their own; and his overwhelming desire to prove himself a brave, courageous leader, I have read.

His argumentative and illiterate mother, Mary Washington, didn't think much of her little boy. She refused to participate in any ceremony honoring little Georgie, and always claimed being neglected. To George's embarrassment she asked the Virginia legislature, at the height of the Revolutionary War, to come to her financial aid.

George was himself quite meticulous when it came to watching his pennies. Though he asked for no salary as Revolutionary General or as President, his expense accounts are a topic of a good deal of historical inquiry. There are those who contend that it might have been cheaper to pay him a salary after all.

Some letters show that he may have had a little thing going with a neighbor's wife, a Mrs. Sally Fairfax. Of course if he was actually impotent, it would have been a very little thing, I'd imagine.

One notion does seem to be certain though. George Washington was a brave and fearless warrior. How smart, bright, or tactical a warrior he was, may be another matter. His best tactic was getting beat, but yet surviving long enough to escape overnight in order to come back again to fight on another day. He does appear to be a lucky guy who led a rather charmed life. His marriage to the chubby, affable little widow Martha, made him just about if not, the richest man in the Colonies.

You could say that he was lucky in marriage, lucky in war, and lucky in business, but the truth is he sought out each in a planned determined way.

When he decided to be married, he rode all over the state proposing to any super-rich widow who might have him. In his business he was watchful and meticulous. In war he was brave, courageous, determined, and if not the smartest, a man who learned well from his mistakes.

His greatest fame comes not from what he did, but from what he didn't do. He was a military leader who won a revolution and didn't attempt a permanent takeover of power after his victory. Unlike Cromwell, Napoleon, Lenin or Mao Zedong, Castro and who knows who else throughout history, he walked away from the seat of power, and had to be lured back and even begged to take a second term as a lowly president never mind King or Caesar, or his Royal Majesty.

This may not seem to be much but it stands as unique in the annals of human history. And if he didn't take the reins for those first few years, it does seem that this Republic - for which it stands - might never have come about.

Interesting

Characters

John Brown (1800-1859)

John Brown was a white abolitionist (anti-slavery advocate) who was hung by the neck until dead in the year 1859. He became a symbol for the cause of the abolitionist and was made into a folk hero of sorts by many prominent writers and the people of his day.

Henry David Thoreau, Ralph Waldo Emerson, and the famous attorney for the damned, Clarence Darrow, all wrote of John Brown in glowing terms. "One of the purest and bravest and highest-minded patriots of any age," says Clarence Darrow. Clarence goes on to compare John Brown with other famous personages of the past, among them: Oliver Cromwell, Mahomet, John Calvin, and even Jesus Christ.

John Brown may have a legitimate comparison with John Calvin, Mahomet, and Oliver Cromwell, but John Brown was no Jesus Christ. John Brown was no advocate of peace. John Brown is quoted as saying that if any man came between him and what he felt to be the will of his God, he would kill him. John Brown was a murderer. John Brown is a man that took the law into his own hands, made himself the judge and jury and without any right to appeal, he slaughtered people as he saw fit.

Clarence Darrow claims that John Brown was doing God's work, the work of programmed destiny. He was fighting the abomination of slavery. This sounds rather ludicrous coming from a man who in another essay gives one of the most cogent defenses of atheism that I have ever read.

Lawrence Kansas, a non-slave community, was sacked and burnt to the ground by a band of bandits who advocated slavery. In Washington D.C. in 1856 an abolitionist Senator by the name of Charles Sumner was nearly beaten to death on the Senate floor by a pro-slave advocate, Senator Andrew Butler. John Brown, incensed by these atrocities, decided that revenge was justice. He and his sons with knives and sabers in hand went on a killing spree. Their goal was to kill any pro-slavers in their neighborhood. And if they happened to get an innocent person by mistake, here and there, oh well nobody's perfect.

John Brown then decided that the only way to solve this slavery problem was by way of war and/or revolution. He decided to raid the arsenal at Harper's Ferry, steal all the weapons, start his own army and overthrow the government. Ironically he was subdued in this effort by Colonel Robert E. Lee.

If you like John Brown and his methods, then you would probably also like some of these people today who in the name of Jesus go around blowing up abortion clinics or shooting doctors through their kitchen windows in front of their wives and children. You would probably also like the Oklahoma bomber, and other terrorist who kill first and ask for justice later. History is full of murders and killers who think that the end justifies the means.

John Brown was no Jesus Christ. He was no Mahatma Gandhi. He was no Martin Luther King. He was a man filled with murder, hate, self-righteousness, and religious fanaticism. The problems, injustices, and hatreds promoted by slavery were not solved by the violence of John Brown or by the Civil War for that matter. As far as I can see no war in history has ever solved the problems and disagreements that precipitated them. Minds must be informed, enlightened and convinced in order to produce change. Beatings, bombs and bullets just don't seem to hold up under the tests of time. If John Brown was a hero then I suppose Osama bin Laden is also.

General Smedley Darlington Butler (1881-1940)

The Plot to Seize the White House

This book written by Jules Archer is basically a biography of General Smedley D. Butler.

General Butler was quite well-known in his day. The plot he exposed to seize the White House was investigated by Congress.

Smedley Butler was a Marine and quite a Marine he was. He is another great General from a Quaker background. At his death, he was the most decorated Marine in U.S. History. His book *War is a Racket* is still being circulated today. His dad was a judge and served in the Congress for 32 years.

Smedley fought in Cuba, in the Philippines, in Mexico, in Nicaragua, in Honduras, in Granada, in Haiti, in China, and in Europe during World War I. He served in the Marine Corps for 33 years and on August 21, 1931 in a speech before the American Legion convention in Connecticut he summed up his career with the following:

"I spent 33 years ... being a high class muscle man for Big Business, for Wall Street and the bankers. In short I was a racketeer for capitalism ... I helped purify Nicaragua for the international banking house of Brown Brothers in 1909-1912. I helped make Mexico and especially Tampico safe for American oil interests in 1916. I brought light to the Dominican Republic for American sugar interests in 1916. I helped make Haiti and Cuba a decent place for the National City [Bank] boys to collect revenue in. I helped in the rape of half a dozen Central American republics for the benefit of Wall Street.

"In China in 1927 I helped see to it that Standard Oil went its way unmolested ... I had ... a swell racket. I was rewarded with honors, medals, promotions ... I might have given Al Capone a few hints. The best he could do was operate a racket in three cities. The Marines operated on three continents."

And he went on.

As you can imagine he created quite a stir. But his Marines loved him. They lined up everywhere to hear him speak and to shake his hand. He was under fire over 120 times in his career, wounded numerous times and had a chest full of medals. He was presented with the prestigious Medal of Honor twice. On the first presentation he sent it back saying that he didn't deserve it. The Marine Corps returned his medal and ordered him to wear it. So he did.

At his retirement at Quantico he gave his farewell speech to his beloved Leathernecks and said; "It has been a privilege to scrap for you just as you have scrapped for me ... When I leave I mean to give every one of you a map showing you exactly where I live. I want you to come around and see me, especially if you ever get into trouble and I will help you if I can. I can give you a square meal and a place to sleep even if I can not guarantee you a political job."

He actually gave out maps and it is said that he lived up to all his promises.

He supported the 1932 Bonus Army and their march on Washington and the Hover government. This was the same group of World War I vets who were routed out of their cardboard shacks and tents by MacArthur, Eisenhower, and Patton brandishing their sabers and doing their "duty" to defend America against America's past heroes.

General Butler supported Franklin Roosevelt and he had this to say in one of his speeches:

"Today, with all our wealth, a deathly gloom hangs over us. Today we appear to be divided. There has developed, through the past few years, a new Tory class, a group that believes that the Nation, its resources and its manpower was provided by the Almighty for its own special use and profit ... on the other side is the great mass of American people who still believe in the Declaration of Independence and the Constitution of the United States.

"This Tory group, through its wealth, its power and its influence, has obtained a firm grip on our government to the detriment of our people and the wellbeing of our Nation. We will prove to the world that we meant what we said a century and a half ago - that this government was instituted not only to secure to our people the rights of life, liberty, and the pursuit of happiness but the right to eat and to all our willing millions the right to work."

He developed a unique military strategy. He shook the press and all the big wigs when he said that he would never again carry a gun on foreign soil. He went on to propose two Constitutional Amendments. In the first he suggested that only those who were physically able to fight be allowed to vote on any war. In the second he suggested that our planes and ships guard our coastline exclusively. He wanted it to be an end to U.S. imperialism and foreign wars. He was even opposed to our entry into World War II.

This book then goes on to tell of a plot on the part of the disgruntled rich and wealthy in America to seize the U.S. Government via an organization of soldiers and World War I veterans and establish a fascist government - just as had been done in Italy and Germany. Butler exposed the plot and named names - the DuPonts, J. P. Morgan, Rockefeller, Pew, Mellon, Al Smith, John J. Raskob and others of the rich and prominent were all brought under the spotlight.

An investigation in Congress took place and, of course, all the charges were denied. No one was ever indicted or prosecuted, but all of Butler's claims were verified and corroborated by the investigators. The plot was foiled by its exposure and the American people and its government was alerted to the danger.

James Carville (1944-)

I'm sure that you all know James Carville. Mr. Carville is a leftwing apologist for the Democratic Party. He was in the Clinton administration. He is a baldheaded, rather blunt, outspoken guy.

I read one of his books awhile ago and I thought that he did a rather good job in explaining why he was a Democrat and a supporter of the Democratic Philosophy. But I no longer take Mr. Carville seriously. The reason that I no longer take Mr. Carville seriously is because he married Mary Madalin. Mary Madalin is a rightwing apologist for the Republican Party.

Now I know what you are thinking. You think that I am a bigot or that I take my politics too seriously. But that is not the case at all. My opinion is not based on politics; it is based on simple, unadulterated common sense.

James Carville married Mary Madalin when he was a mature adult - not when he was a youth still in the processes of social, physical and political maturation. He was a full grown mature adult Democrat. His wife was also full grown and Republican. They have no excuse for this type behavior.

There are people living in this country who think it a perversion for the members of different races to "intermingle." There are others who consider it a perversion for members of the same sex to marry. Well, it is an equal perversion for Democrats and Republicans to interbreed. This is clearly overstepping the bounds of the sanctity of philosophical integrity. Anyone who believes in and cherishes philosophy knows that Democrats and Republicans can not marry. I mean think of the psychologically disfigured children that must result from such a union? This is pure and simple child abuse. These type people should be locked up and the key thrown away. This is criminal and socially irresponsible - not to mention a complete bastardization and mongrelizing of cultural, philosophical genetics.

Being a Democratic or a Republican is not a learned or thought out phenomenon. It is genetic - it is predetermined by Creation. You don't evolve into a Democrat or a Republican - you are born that way. It is like the color of your skin or your physical structure as a male or a female. You do not choose to be a Democrat or a Republican you are born one or the other - whether you realize or understand it or not. Living in a household of mixed political parentage only confuses the poor little Democrats and Republicans. The poor little half breed Repubocrats end up cheating on their wives while wearing bow ties or trying to find charitable investments on the stock market. They go through life trying to rationalize the notion that GE or DuPont are "green." The poor little things wander around bowling alleys looking for collectibles or trying to establish nude stamp collections. It is worse than being an Idiot Savant.

Many Republicans go through life thinking that they are Democrats and many Democrats live just the opposite type of confused misguided existence. This type confusion is much worse than what is termed as a "sexual identity crisis." It is much worse than "passing for white" in the black community. It is a complete disconnect from what Creation intended and those that live in this state cannot be saved. Unfortunately they will not go to heaven; they will never see their Creator and their life here on earth will be a living hell and furthermore they will not be allowed to pass "go" nor will they be entitled to collect two hundred dollars. In fact living life as a Democrat when you were born a Republican is hell right here on this earth and vise versa.

Obviously Mr. Carville and his bride don't know what the heck they are and really shouldn't be listened to by anybody with any common sense.

Now once again you say to yourself, Well, I'll bet that this man writing this article is not always in agreement with his wife. So what the heck is he talking about?

That is very true, but I have a justifiable excuse. When my wife and I met, we were both lost in the throes of sexual delusion. We were not mature. We had never given a second thought to our innate genetic propensities – other than you know what. My wife has "learned" to disagree with me for her own health and psychological protection, just as I have learned over the course of thirty years that she is basically a child, as are all women, who should be seen and not heard.

But we didn't know this when we first met. My god how stupid could one possibly be? Do you think that my wife would have married me if she knew then what her life would be from

123

that day forward? Do you think that she is a complete fool? Why do you think that they demand in the wedding ceremony that the two sexually intoxicated volunteers agree to take vows demanding loyalty in the future? This has been going on for a long time. The people in charge of these things know what is happening.

Mr. Carville and Mary Madalin, being mature adults, knew from day one and they moved forward and even went so far as to reproduce. This is a total horror story. Their children will one day be the subjects of a special 48 Hours. I have no doubt.

So, in conclusion, it is one thing to listen to and take advice from people who have done their best to promote a delusion of sanity to others when underneath they are truly as nutty as a bedbug – the Clinton's or Bush's for example. But when two people display for you - right before your own eyes their complete and unadulterated instability and mental degradation - why would anyone in their apparent right mind listen to these people?

I am happy that these two have been able to provide for themselves and they have not become a burden to the state or the taxpayers but shouldn't they be doing something as an occupation in this society that is not detrimental to the public good?

I suppose if we can have some of the people that we have had as presidents of this United States we can have a few more loony-toones as TV political advisers and analysts - what additional harm could it possibly do? I mean they aren't the crazies who are actually making the decisions - they are just commenting on the decisions made by the crazies in charge. And what is more important is that we don't really have to listen to any of them. Unlike presidents, dictators and other various tyrants we can ignore what the Carvilles and others of their ilk have to say without losing our citizenship or subjecting our future to torture, imprisonment, starvation, water-boarding or being hit by a semi-guided missile or anything like that.

Silas Deane vs Tom Paine

My interest in this story was peaked by a book entitled *After the Fact –The Art of Historical Detection.*

Silas Deane was born in Groton, Connecticut. His father was only a blacksmith but he managed to get the boy to Yale where Silas received his law degree. Silas was a very ambitious young man. He married well, not once, but twice. His first bride was a widow and her late husband was merchant. Silas took over the business. After his first wife died he met and married the granddaughter of a former governor of Connecticut. This must have peeked Silas's interest in politics. He became a delegate to the first and second Continental Congress.

In 1776 Congress sent Deane to France. He was the first American to represent the American Colonies abroad. He also had a rather clandestine mission. The Americans wanted him to purchase war materials and arms for the upcoming battle. In France, he was secretly hooked up with a playwright, named Beaumarchais and a dummy company called Hortalez and Company. The French were on shaky terms with the British. They wanted no publicity with regards to their helping British Colonies to revolt. The French King was not ready for a war with England at the moment.

Beaumarchais ... "The courtly gentleman of 'wit and genius'" as Deane called him, sold gunpowder to Americans at a 500 percent markup and sent bills of lading with the shipments indicating these were not gifts. Muskets discarded by the French army and given to Beaumarchais for nothing were passed along to the United States at half their original cost. Robert Morris, another well known Patriot, told Deane before he left Philadelphia ... "If we have but luck in getting the goods safe to America the profits will be sufficient to content us all." Late in 1777 Congress got the bill from Hortalez and Company for 4,500,000 livres. It was authorized by Deane. The Congress decided to call Deane home for a talk.

Congress, through the year 1778 had been having difficulty with scandals of a similar nature. A Dr. William Shippen, head of the medical department, seemed to have a good deal of extra money from his negotiations in hospital supplies. Then there was Thomas Mifflin an army quartermaster-general who had done a little too well at his post. And good old General Nathanael Green was rumored to be making a rather quick fortune. "By late 1778 the American Revolution for many had lost the quality of a crusade. Those who had prospered on wartime contracts now rolled about Philadelphia in gaudy coaches.

While the ragged continental army survived on half rations, slim supplies and often no pay, the city's rich, many of them friends of Deane, dressed their women in finery and loaded their tables with delicacies. John Adams was worried. He feared that the publicity from all these money scandals and profiteering could result in an actual civil war."

Deane had a couple of other scams going at the time. Deane would use his political connections in France to ship goods without declaring what the cargo was. If the ship would arrive safely, he would declare it private - his personal goods. If the ship sunk, or the goods were damaged, he would declare it a U.S. government cargo. On top of that he had a gambling problem. Some of the more interesting gambling casinos of the day were the insurance companies.

The insurance companies would insure anything. They would even give you odds on current events. You could "insure" yourself on the possibility of an upcoming war, or who might win or lose the present war. Deane, being an insider in the political shenanigans going on between France and the Colonies, had been doing quite well in many of his "insurance" ventures.

When Deane got back home a big brouhaha erupted. The inspectors asked to see the account books, only to find that Deane had "forgotten" them in Europe. Tom Paine who had proudly taken the position of Secretary for Foreign Affairs to Congress in the American War, at no pay I might add, had privileged information in his files. These privileged files clearly stated that the King of France had donated the bulk of these materials to the Colonial war effort, free of charge. When Tom pointed this out to the investigating committee, he was called a liar. Deane not only called Tom Paine a liar, but he went to the newspapers with his side of the story. Paine demanded an apology from Deane. When Deane refused, Paine went to the newspapers himself. Deane then demanded an apology and a retraction from Paine. Paine proceeded to document his allegation to the committee and the newspapers with information from his privileged files. This mess caused the president of the Congress, Henry Laurens, to resign and the French ambassador, Mr. Gerard, to have convulsions.

Now Mr. Gerard entered the committee room and the newspaper columns. He demanded that Paine denounce all such accusation about his beloved France and its proper King. The French government would never, never do such a thing, and certainly not the King. In private, Mr. Gerard was not at all upset with Mr. Paine. He even offered to put Tom on the French payroll as a propagandist for French causes in the Colonies. In public, though, he was hot.

Paine had annoyed a number of other people besides Mr. Gerard; both Robert and Gouverneur Morris where not happy with Tommy. Gouvernouer Morris was a friend of Deane and Tommy had insinuated that such notables as Robert Morris might actually be in on some of the ill-gotten gain themselves. Paine was asked to resign. Paine resigned from the committee, but he did not resign as a journalist. He continued to defend himself and attacked publicly several prominent members of the committee who had forced his resignation; Gouvernor Morris, John Penn, William Drayton, and others.

Paine was disgraced and ostracized and Deane went back to France. As Deane bumped about Europe, he was approached by the British to write home to some of his influential friends encouraging the Colonies to capitulate with the British. The British double-crossed Deane and had the letters printed in occupied New York. Immediately Deane became a traitor and Paine, once again a hero. Deane was forced to remain in Europe. He took to alcohol and most likely gambling. He went broke. Finally, after a number of years, a relative in the Colonies agreed to pay his passage home. He died mysteriously aboard the ship. Some say he committed suicide; others say that he was poisoned. If he was poisoned, it was probably by a guy named Edward Bancroft who is alleged to have been a double agent.

Bancroft was an old friend. They were involved in many an "insurance" deal together. Bancroft had done quite well in the espionage game and may not have wanted the publicity that an old, wimpy, soul searching Deane might have engaged in upon returning to his homeland.

Henry Ford (1863-1947)

Henry Ford is one of those positive/negative type guys. No sooner do you read something good about him than you pick up something else that paints him as a demon.

Positive: Henry manufactured an automobile, by an assembly line process, paid his workers an astounding five dollars a day, and produced an automobile that even the workers in his factories could afford to buy. He was a popular national and world hero - a super-wealthy capitalist but yet, the champion of the wage earner and the working class.

Negative: His assembly line process was a stab in the back to craftsmanship and the organized labor force of the day. His system reduced the laborer to a machine. Any bonehead could work on his assembly line, no skilled labor required. His assembly lines were sophisticated, modern, industrialized torture chambers.

He paid five dollars a day not because he was a generous man and wanted to improve the plight of the workingman but because he couldn't get anybody to work at his boring, monotonous, regimented factory assembly line for more than a short period of time. People felt the work demeaning, and insulting to their intelligence.

No worker at the factory was allowed to learn the whole process, therefore hampering anyone from working for Henry for a year or two and then opening up an Oldsmobile plant in the neighborhood.

Positive: Henry was a peace loving man who advocated against World War I. At one point, he actually sent some sort of peace ship to Europe, the Oscar II, in hope of preventing or stopping the war. He didn't believe in charity, but paid generously and even over paid for items that he wanted to collect for his famous museum - a kindhearted capitalist.

Negative: Somewhere along the assembly line Henry determined that the Jews were the curse of mankind. He published a newspaper out of Dearborn, Michigan through which he "informed" the general public of a "Jewish Conspiracy" to take over the world. He went so far as to publish and distribute this notion throughout the world. Henry

Ford is credited with pumping out more anti-Jewish literature and negative propaganda in the 1920's than Adolf Hitler.

It is said by historian William Manchester that Adolf Hitler had Henry as one of his idols, distributed Henry's book, *The International Jew*, at the Reichstag and had Henry's picture in his jail cell (imprisonment resulting from the 1923 putsch). Henry was to become Hitler's North American dictator once Hitler conquered the world.

Researchers today are finding links between Henry and Adolf that amount to more than ideology. James Pool in *Who Financed Hitler* devotes a whole chapter to the connection between Henry and Adolf. In *Trading with the Enemy* by Charles Higham, Henry and the Ford Motor Company are significant. In *Hitler and His Secret Partners - 1933-1945* again by James Pool, Henry Ford is also considered. But the most recent and extensive book on Henry, Hitler and Nazism that I have read is *The American Axis* by Max Wallace. This book deals with both Henry Ford and Charles Lindbergh and their ties with Adolf Hitler and Nazism. If we can believe all the accusations and information in this book, FDR's famous statement with regards to Charles Lindbergh being a Nazi could certainly be expanded to include Henry Ford.

Many others accuse Henry along with Thomas Edison, Lucky Lindy and many more wealthy Americans and Europeans of financially backing Adolf in his rise to power. The wealthy all over the world were very much distressed by the antics of the anti-Capitalist, Russian Bolsheviks and others who were in the process of "redistributing" wealth and encouraging the mass burial of a lot of once respected entrepreneurs and royalty.

Reinhard Gehlen (1902-1979)

If you have never heard of Reinhard Gehlen, join the club. He was the head of the German Nazi secret intelligence service, eastern division. Believe it or not, instead of being hung by the neck until dead, or given the firing squad after World War II for his many crimes against humanity, he and his friends were incorporated into a new spying organization established in 1947 by the Truman administration - the C.I.A. Harry Truman has since denounced the C.I.A. as one of his biggest mistakes.

Gehlen had microfilmed his Russian spy records and buried them somewhere in the mountains in Germany. He negotiated with the invading Americans and attempted to trade his files, information, friends and connections, for his life. He not only saved his sorry butt, but got him and his friends put on the U.S. payroll.

One of his friends was a Doctor Franz Six, a convicted war criminal who was sentenced to twenty years in prison at the Nuremberg trails. Benjamin Fenercz, a U.S. prosecutor at Nuremberg, said that Six was one of the biggest "swine" in the whole mobile killing squad cases. Six served about four years and then was given clemency by the U.S. high commissioner in Germany, John McCloy.

John McCloy had a penchant for releasing and pardoning Nazi murderers, killers, industrialist and German arms manufacturers who were guilty of manufacturing weapons by working tens of thousands of slave laborers to their death. McCloy's name keeps popping up in history books, most notably as one of the appointments to the infamous Warren Commission.

Doctor Emil Augsburg who ended up as a Porsche Agent by 1961, another one of Gehlen's friends, was involved in mass murder and the assassination of German Jews.

It is interesting to me that while my dad, and possibly yours, was being laid-off from his job shortly after World War II, the United States Government somehow found two hundred million dollars to employ 4,000 ex-Nazi murders to help Reinhard Gehlen resurrect "the Org."

Reinhard Gehlen's career is not a secret. I have, right here in front of me, the memoirs of Reinhard Gehlen entitled, *The*

Service, and another book entitled *Blowback* by Christopher Simpson which highlights Gehlen's career and the careers of many of his friends and associates.

Reinhard, along with being credited with the torture and murder of tens of thousands in his information gathering days, is said to have been one of the major influences behind the postwar American anti-Communist paranoia, McCarthyism, and even the Cold War itself.

If you have been reading about American C.I.A. agents torturing women and children in South America and elsewhere, and have considered it all a bunch of bull, you might want to take a look at the life of one of your paid government employees, Reinhard Gehlen, and some of his German Nazi friends in "the Org." You might find the life and times of Allen Dulles, brother of Secretary of State John Foster Dulles equally interesting.

Oh, by the way, Allen Dulles the man responsible for the Bay of Pigs fiasco as the director of the C.I.A. and fired (retired) shortly thereafter by John F. Kennedy, was also an appointee to the Warren Commission. Funny, they just picked his name out of a hat, I guess.

Alexander Hamilton (1755/57-1806)

Alexander Hamilton is another confusing and controversial character in the history of the United States Government. Alexander certainly cannot be considered a believer in democratic rule or democracy as defined as; of the people, by the people and for the people.

As our present system and popular prejudices exhibit, we have two types of democrats. The first is that type individual who places his confidence in the notion that the masses of people will come to a proper understanding of the affairs of the nation and will instinctively choose the proper leadership or the proper course of action. He places his confidence in all of the people and the theory that truth, justice and the American way will somehow ring through their providential voices.

The second type democrat does not believe that the masses are truly capable. He believes that their mass voice will not ring with providential truth but chaos. He suggests that they must be guided, directed and in some instances forced to follow the proper conclusion. Some would say that this type person is not a democrat.

In our present system we define both these types as believers in democracy. And both of our present day political parties are of the second category in my opinion. Both the Democrats and the Republicans are republicans.

Alexander was even more republican than are all our Republicans of today. He certainly didn't believe that all men were created equal, or that they should be treated equally. And though he was, maybe, the most significant individual in getting the Constitution ratified among the various States/Colonies, he wasn't really that heavy on the American Constitution himself. But he did believe that America needed a government and the Constitution was a step in the right direction.

America also needed a government with a means of defending itself, exercising power over its own people, and with a controlled financial ability.

He fought for the establishment of the Colonies as an independent nation and served in the initial stabilizing, and government of George Washington.

He was a money man who favored big business, strong central government, and rule by the few over the many. He was George Washington's right hand man in the war and in his government.

He was an elitist with a not very elite background. He was illegitimate, poor, received his education by a grant of charity from friends and neighbors who chipped in and sent him from the islands to the mainland to be educated. He is also credited to be a man of outstanding character, but had seemingly no qualms about cheating on his wife and their eight children; or using his financial position to seduce another man's young attractive wife.

His financial dealings were under constant suspicion and scrutiny, and he once told Thomas Jefferson that corruption was a necessary part of proper government.

He is also the author of a number of vary suspicious love letters. They are most suspicious because they were written to a male friend.

If I wrote all of this while Alexander was still alive, he would, most likely, have challenged me to a duel. But I wouldn't have been stupid enough to use his father-in-laws hair-trigger, rigged, dueling pistols; though Aaron Burr seems to have been successful, but then again maybe Aaron brought his own pistol.

It is claimed by some that Alexander actually shot first and intentionally missed his target, but Burr declined to extend the courtesy.

Doctor Armand Hammer (1898-1990)

Armand Hammer (not Arm & Hammer) must be one of the most amazing businessmen who ever lived. Reading his lifetime accomplishments and his choice in decisions leaves one gasping. There must be business people in the world today who brag, as sports enthusiasts once did with regards to John L. Sullivan, "This is the hand that shook the hand of Armand Hammer."

It was said about Tom Paine that one could see genius in his eyes. As I look into the eyes of the pictures of Tom Paine and Armand Hammer, it seems to me, as it is with almost everyone else, that with my own preconceptions I can make them whatever I want them to be.

I can see Armand Hammer as a young enthusiastic idealist in Bolshevik Russia, or as a scheming chairman of the board in uptown, downtown corporate America. But then I can put a T-shirt on the man, and a can of beer in his hand and see him sitting on the front porch in my old neighborhood jabbering in the old tongue to some newly arrived immigrants. I am afraid that with geniuses, it is as it is said to be with thieves - it takes one to know one. And obviously I am not qualified.

Armand Hammer, probably one of the most successful capitalists ever, had a dad who was a convicted Socialist agitator here in America. He went to prison. He was convicted of performing illegal abortions. He served his time but was later exonerated.

Armand Hammer sold the first tractors ever to set tread on Russian soil to arch communist Russian, anti-Capitalist immortal, Nikolai Lenin. Not only that, they were Ford tractors. Henry Ford was one of the biggest, richest capitalist and haters of communism, bolshevism and organized labor who ever lived.

Armand Hammer, believe it or not, convinced Henry Ford to build a factory in Russia from which Henry Ford made tens, if not hundreds of millions of dollars via Russian Communist Rubles. If this doesn't seem astounding enough, add to the equation that Armand Hammer was of Jewish ancestry. Henry

Ford was a vicious anti-Semite who at the very moment of these negotiations was putting out a newspaper in Dearborn Michigan exposing a ficticious Jewish conspiracy to control the world.

Henry Ford, it is said by historians, was one of Adolf Hitler's idols. Adolf supposedly had Henry's picture hanging on the wall in his jail cell in 1923.

Armand Hammer built an economic empire valued into the hundreds of billions of dollars. And he went from pharmaceuticals to asbestos, to pencils, to tractors, to antiques and collectable; from museums to department stores, to oil, to livestock; from one political system to another; from dictator to democrats, from communists to capitalists as if they were all one and the same. Andrew Carnegie had nothing on this guy. I've got to read more on Armand Hammer. I hope he wrote an autobiography.

Alger Hiss (1904-1996)

The first thing that you have to remember about Alger Hiss is that he is not Rudolf Hess. Rudolf Hess is that Nazi guy, who flew to England for some yet to be explained reasons and was tried and convicted at the Nuremberg trails.

Alger Hiss was also tried and convicted, but in the United States, for being a Communist and supplying information to the Russians in 1938.

Alger Hiss was a graduate of Harvard Law school; was a clerk to Supreme Court Justice, Oliver Wendell Homes, Jr.; was one of Franklin D. Roosevelt's bright young men; was in the State Department; served on the Agriculture committee; on the Nye committee investigating improprieties and profiteering in the armament industry; was with Roosevelt at Yalta; served on the international committee which drafted the U.N. charter; and was president of the Carnegie Endowment for International Peace. But, after tangling with McCarthy, Nixon, J. Edgar Hoover and a guy named Whittaker Chambers, he ended up selling paperclips and rubber bands for a living. He was also disbarred and went to prison for nearly four years.

It seems that he spent the remainder of his life trying to clear his name and turn over his 1948 conviction. His biggest mistake, it seems to me, was agreeing to serve on the Nye Commission which was assigned to investigate war profiteering by people like the DuPonts, Curtiss Wright and Pratt & Whitney companies.

Aggravating the DuPonts and others in the armament industry by announcing that the charges against them were fair and justifiable, just as they were during World War I, was not a smart move. And further stating that the only way to end corruption in the armament industry was to end war altogether was just adding insult to injury. When you consider that the DuPonts actually tried to raise a private army to violently overthrow the Roosevelt administration ... come on now?

Franklin and Harry Hopkins were now dead. The Stalin connection was over. Harry Truman was having tea with the old Clividen set and the entire world was reinvesting in Krupp Industries.

This was not a time to be investigating war profiteers. It is also interesting to consider why we spent so much time investigating communists after the war, as opposed to Nazi sympathizers. After all, I don't mean to shock anybody, but the commies, both Russian and Chinese, were our allies, and the Nazis were our enemies.

In Alger Hiss' last book, *Recollections of a Life,* Alger makes his last plea for exoneration, and he makes a very, very good case. He had been anxiously awaiting files to be released under the Freedom of Information Act which were guaranteed to take no more than ten days. It took four and a half years. Oh well?

In any case, information from the newly released Russian files, supposedly contradicts Alger's testimony once again. I wish Alger was still around to defend himself on this one, but now he is dead also.

Recently the debate has reappeared. The adopted son of the Hisses, Timothy Hobson, has advanced Alger's innocence once again. He and his half brother Tony Hiss - who dedicated his life to clearing his dad's name - are proclaiming Alger Hiss's conviction to have been a blatant tragedy perpetrated by a series of lies and falsifications.

Timothy, a ten year old in 1937 and a household witness to any supposed spying or espionage was not allowed to testify in defense of his parents at the trial in 1947 because he had received an Undesirable Discharge from the military on the grounds that he was a homosexual.

What is truly unbelievable is that Alger Hiss and this single case marks a turning point in the politics of the American people.

When Alger Hiss was convicted of perjury (not espionage or treason) America turned from the liberalism of FDR and his pro-Russian, anti-German/Nazism position to the Cold War pro-German/Marshall Plan, anti-Russian Bolshevik position. This poor man and this tragic case are like the linchpin in one of the biggest policy changes and turnarounds in all of American History. Talk about being in the wrong place at the wrong time!

Robert Green Ingersoll (1833-1899)

"The Great Agnostic"

Robert G. Ingersoll is touted as being possibly the greatest public speaker in American history. When we think of past great speakers like Mark Twain, Abraham Lincoln, Frederick Douglas, Daniel Webster, William Jennings Bryan, Billy Sunday, Stephan A. Douglas and Clarence Darrow one must be tempted to say ... Robert Inger-who? Is somebody making a joke here? But nevertheless I read this claim being made over and over in book after book. I don't know what to say and since I have never heard any of these men speak, I will never know.

Mr. Ingersoll who is labeled as "the Great Agnostic" characterizes himself as an atheist. He was the son of a Congregationalist minister.

Robert's family was not wealthy and they did not come into wealth. Nevertheless Robert became super wealthy. Because of his latter fame in speaking against the Bible, God and Christianity one is led to believe that he made his fortune lecturing on these subjects.

Not true. He and his brother Clark both became lawyers in the old fashioned way - they passed a bar exam. Neither of them had any education to speak of and very little training at law - but they took the bar exam and passed. From then on, they seemed to be blessed - but by who or what they did not know and did not care.

They opened their own law firm, got involved in politics and the railroad business and the money rolled in. By the time Robert started on his very successful career as a public speaker he was already exceptionally rich.

He was a very sought after speaker. He lectured on Tom Paine, politics, social issues and history along with his anti-religious agenda. His remuneration for his speeches ranged between $400 and $7,000 per engagement which in today's money was up to $50,000 per lecture. Believe it or not Mark Twain was a warm-up speaker for the likes of Robert Ingersoll.

He became a super success as a lawyer defending the railroad robber barons of the later 1800's and then added to his fortune by marrying Eva Weld Parker, daughter of the very wealthy Benjamin Weld Parker of Tazewell County in Illinois.

Robert Ingersoll spoke out freely and without much reservation against God and religion especially in the later part of his career. One would think due to the propagandizing going on today that Mr. Ingersoll was a forerunner of that dreadful class of individuals known and hated as "liberals." But as unfortunate as this may be Robert was a conservative Republican. It is difficult to imagine a Republican or a conservative in today's world who does not believe in the absolute truth of superstition and historical fable but the Republican Robert G. Ingersoll was one.

He fought in the Civil War for the North. He was at the battle of Shiloh. He was taken captive near Corinth in Tennessee. He was sent to St. Louis, Missouri and exchanged. After that he admitted to having seen enough of the "bloodshed and humiliation" of war and resigned his commission. From that time forward he provided good example for many others by only preaching the honor and glory of war while avoiding any active participation.

He did eventually support Abraham Lincoln (after first agreeing with Stephan A. Douglas) but never totally with regards to Lincoln's Emancipation Proclamation. He felt that blacks in America should be sent to live in their own country – somewhere else on the planet.

He was slow to come around to women's suffrage and though a multi-millionaire back in the days when a million was a million, he didn't spend very much of his fortune on his daughters' education. He had two girls. One he named Eva Robert and the other Maud Robert.

He was not in favor of Trade Unionism or of anyone protesting against the political order. He is quoted to have said in an interview with *The Mail* and *Express*, New York, November 3, 1887: "There is no place in this country for the Anarchist. The source of power here is the people, and to attack the political power is to attack the people. If the laws are oppressive, it is the fault of the oppressed. If the laws touch the poor and leave them without redress, it is the fault of the poor."

Interestingly enough, I think this was the basic philosophy that evolved in the Russian Communist system.

Since the Russian system was established by the poor workingman, the Russian government claimed that poor workingmen had no need or right to organize or protest against the government since they were the government. Mr. Ingersol said that since us Americans live in a democratic government of the people, by the people and for the people, the people then have no right to complain. If there is anything wrong, it is their fault, after all, they are "the people."

Unfortunately this is the same philosophy by which Osama bin Laden justifies blowing up innocent people in America and elsewhere. Since we are all a part and thus supportive of our governments, we are all enemy soldiers in his war for social justice.

But, nevertheless, Robert G. Ingersoll was a very rich, outspoken, Republican, conservative atheist who fought in the Civil War but didn't want to free the slaves; who believed in freedom, equality, and equal rights - except for women, blacks, those who spoke out against the political system, and the poor; who believed and advocated war - but would rather have others fight it. He was against the repeal of the Comstock Laws which were used to prohibit the distribution of birth control information via the postal system. He also had a reputation for public intoxication and drunken brawling. He had political aspirations but was not supported because of his unorthodox religious views.

It is clear that Robert felt very strongly about religion - or should we say his lack of religion. But he exhibited little strength of character on any other issues, moral or otherwise. This man could have made a good American President then and now. One has to wonder why he was so determinedly un-conservative when it came to God, the Bible and Christianity. Certainly with a little less courage on this one issue he could have been a famous name in the annals of history - a legend right up there in the ranks of Herbert Hoover, Warren Gambrel Harding, Calvin Coolidge, Ronald Reagan, George Herbert Walker Bush and George W. Bush. What a shame - a good conservative whose only legacy is his exceptional wealth and his disbelief in God, the Bible and Christianity.

Joseph P. Kennedy (1888-1969)

As Albert Einstein exemplified, perspective is a fascinating phenomenon. Being raised in the greater Boston, Massachusetts area maybe I can present a slightly different picture of that big S.O.B., Joseph P. Kennedy. My oral and street education went something like this.

Joseph P. Kennedy was the product of poor, Irish-immigrant, Catholic heritage. The Irish were basic European waste matter. "Send in the Irish," was the typical British, military chant whenever they had a situation that required a waste of human life.

In the pre-civil war days of the U.S., the Irish were used where slave owners feared to tread. An Irishmen's life at ten cents a day was a much better buy than a black slave who may have cost his owner five hundred to fifteen hundred dollars.

With this as his background, Joseph P. Kennedy committed the gravest of sins. He became one of the richest men in America. And how did he do that?

Well, for one thing, it seems that during the Depression when all of the wealthy established white Anglo-Saxon protestant conservatives were selling out the U.S. as fast as they could, shipping one hundred thousand dollars in gold bars out of the country each week, that S.O.B., Kennedy, was risking every penny he had buying up abandoned America as fast as he could. He bought closed factories and discontinued breweries (alcohol, an Irish Catholic traditional beverage that he knew would never die) and everything else that he could get his hands on. He became so knowledgeable of the stock market and all of its shenanigans that he was hired by the Yellow Cab Company to save their butt. He locked himself in a room with a bank of telephones and a bunch of ticker tape machines and by out-playing all the better bunch at their own game he saved the Yellow Cab Company and the jobs of their thousands of workers.

He went on to volunteer to patch up the loopholes in the stock market for FDR - an act that surely didn't please the crowd who made their fortunes wallowing in those holes, but a job that had been successful up and until this new age of international and domestic swindling. Joe considered this act for FDR his greatest act of patriotism.

After that the big S.O.B. opened up his own neighborhood bank, and loaned money to poor Irishmen who would never have gotten a dime elsewhere to buy homes and businesses. His bank prospered and grew and he became one of the super wealthy.

He then went on to inspire his children with the malicious notion that this was the greatest country in the world, where even poor, dumb, maligned, Irishmen could become rich and famous.

Two of these children died in World War II, one in a fighter plane and one by accident. Two of his other boys grew up to have their heads blown off by ungrateful, jealous Americans because of the Kennedy boys' attempts to make their country a better place for all people to live.

There was a time in America when Joseph P. Kennedy would have been considered an American Hero.

So much for perspective?

Charles Lindbergh (1902-1974)

Most of us know of "The Spirit of St. Louis" the airplane; not the ship, the SS St. Louis, that wandered around endlessly without a port for its Jewish cargo who were trying to escape from Nazi Germany in 1939. We know of Bruno Hauptmann and the horrible story of the kidnapping and murder of the Lindbergh's baby, but this is certainly only a tiny part of the Lindbergh story.

Lindbergh unfortunately got into politics. He became one of America's chief back-door supporters of Adolf Hitler and Nazism. He was friends with Herman Goering and a great admirer of Herman's German Luftwaffe (air force). Lindbergh became the chief spokesmen and prominent figure in the America First movement - an isolationist/pro German movement designed to keep the U.S. out of World War II.

Charles Lindbergh helped to train the German Air Force and received the Silver Cross, their medal of honor, for his services - a medal which he refused to return to Germany after they declared war on the United States.

Lindbergh hated Roosevelt. He considered him a Communist living in the White House. Roosevelt said that if Lindbergh was not an American Nazi, nobody was.

When war was declared Lindbergh was denied his commission as an officer in the United States Air Force. He was not allowed to fly or to fight on behalf of this country. At the end of the War, General Eisenhower refused to shake his hand. And a few years later the mayor of Berlin, after Truman's successful Berlin airlift and rescue, refused to appear on the same platform with "that Nazi" Lindbergh.

Lindbergh accused England of being the real European war monger and expressed his hopes that Hitler would eventually conquer Russia and then act as a bulwark against the yellow horde. He had similar unpleasant things to say about the Jews. He said the British, the Jews, and the Roosevelt Government were responsible for World War II.

After war was declared Lindbergh was fired from his prestigious position in the aviation industry, but found employment with Henry Ford.

Henry Ford was attempting to manufacture airplanes to fight his friend Adolf. Henry was pro-Nazi and also a receiver of the German Silver Cross which he too refused to return after war was declared by Germany on the United States. For whatever reasons, Henry Ford and his masterful assembly line technology were not all that successful in assisting the U.S. in its battle against Nazism.

Henry was also responsible for selling the first tractors ever to set tread on Russian Communist soil. It does seem that Henry's main principle and interest was principal and interest.

Lindbergh later became an avid Cold War advocate and supporter of any war against Communism. He was a supporter of both the Korean and Vietnam wars.

In his later life Lindbergh became a conservationist. He adopted tribes of aborigines in the Philippines and Africa and took up to save the planet as a leftist radical environmentalist.

Reverend Thomas Robert Malthus (1766-1834)

Malthus goes down in history as one of the world's greatest thinkers, for writing what I think he considered, the biggest spoof that he had yet concocted, in order to perplex the 'pointy heads' of his day. He presented his essay suggesting to his intellectual adversaries (Godwin, Condorcet and others) that far be it for him to point out what was right before their eyes, but in the spirit of objectivity, maybe they were not quite so blind as he was just dumb. He went on to explain that if one wished to contend that mankind was turning into an Ostrich, reasonable proof should be established corresponding to the notion. Show me some humans with beaks, long necks, and some feathers; it isn't quite enough to simply keep burying your own head into the ground, he mocked.

This bit of sarcasm from his *Essay on the Principle of Population*, which he had published anonymously at first, is in response to Mr. William Godwin's (1756-1836) *An Enquiry Concerning Political Justice*. In his *Enquiry*, Mr. Godwin blames all of the problems in the world onto the WWaspp's or the WWaspc's ... Wealthy, White, Anglo-Saxon Patriotic Protestants or Catholics. Godwin is not quite so specific, but I'm sure Mr. Malthus took it personally.

Godwin contended that the reason all was not right with the world, was because of society and its institutions. But have no fear, all will eventually come around by the natural processes of debate, discussion and enlightenment which will eventually result in the disappearance of all governments, the collapse of all religious tomfoolery, the end to war and pestilence, and the realization on the part of the wealthy that they have too much and should share it with their unfortunate neighbors. So there you go.

Malthus suggested a different proposition. Did you ever think, he suggested and I paraphrase, that the reason that the few have so much and the many so little is that every time Mrs. Many bends over in her garden to plant another row of peas, Mr. Many plants his own seed, thus making Mrs. Many, too Many once again. The perpetuation of this type behavior leads to too many Manyes, and too few peas which then leads to war, famine, pestilence, disease, and mass production (I just threw in that last one, sorry). It is not society, government, God, religion, or even the uneven distribution of wealth. It is simply too many Manyes and too few peas. It is excessive ouuu, ouuu, ouuu, ouuu ... ahhhhhhhhh. Knock off some of the ou-ing and ah-ing and do a little more weeding and all will once again be right with the world. God has a plan. He not only said go out and populate, He said go out and *cultivate* too. Malthus was a minister, you know.

Well, lots of people began reading Malthus' essay. Even some smart people read it, like Darwin and some other scientists, and they weren't laughing. Malthus realized his new found popularity. This ain't bad, he said to himself. So, at the next publication, he not only added to it, but signed his name on it.

The end result of all of this is that the Prime Minister, Billy Pitt, canceled his "Aid to the Poor Bill" and closed down all the soup kitchens around town. Instead of putting a dollar into the poor box, everybody dropped in a condom instead.

Joe McCarthy (1908-1957)

Senator Joseph McCarthy from Wisconsin precipitated hysteria in the United States that rivaled A. Mitchell Palmer and the Wilson administration's "Red Scare."

The word "McCarthyism" was added to our language in his honor. As of this moment, I know of no one, right or left, not even onetime McCarthy defender William F. Buckley Jr., who now classify McCarthy as an honorable character.

He had his own little scandals going with cohort Roy Cohn and Cohn's chum, G. David Schine. Schine was drafted into the Army to the dismay of Cohn - his whispered male sexual partner.

J. Parnell Thomas chaired the House Un-American Activities Committee. Thomas eventually went to jail for payroll padding and taking kickbacks. Richard Nixon and Robert Kennedy were both on the McCarthy payroll at this time also.

During this fiasco many Hollywood celebrities like Robert Montgomery, Ronald Reagan, Adoiphe Menjou, Humphrey Bogart, Jimmy Stewart and a host of others became infamous in leftist circles for ratting on their friends and fellow movie stars.

McCarthy was born on November 15, 1908 on a dairy farm in Appleton, Wisconsin. In 1942 McCarthy, age 35, joined the Marine Corps and received a direct commission as a first lieutenant. In an initiation in honor of the event of crossing the equator, he broke his left foot. A medic removing the cast burnt Joe's leg with some glacial acetic acid. Using this injury, McCarthy evidently forged a letter describing his "heroism" and signed his commanding officer's name to it. This resulted in a citation signed by Admiral Chester Nimitz.

Although Roosevelt won every election handily and always had a Democratic majority in both the house and the Senate, by the time that Truman came along the public was ready for a change. Truman won over Dewey in a real squeaker, but the Democrats lost both the House and the Senate. From then on the Truman administration was under fire. The suggestion that the Democrats had been soft on communism was prevalent all during the Roosevelt years, but with the Republican victories in 1946 and 1948 the poop hit the fan.

Alger Hiss was first on the Republican hit list. Hiss was not convicted of treason or on charges of espionage. He was convicted on December 15, 1948 on two counts of perjury. He had stated in his testimony that he had never turned any documents over to George Crossley (Whittaker Chambers) and that he had not seen Mr. Crossley after Jan. 1, 1937. Hiss was indicted on two counts of perjury.

In a second trial - the first ending in a hung jury - he was convicted. The statute of limitations had run out on any espionage charges against Hiss. The material that he was accused to have secreted to the Russians was deemed harmless and insignificant but yet he was still convicted. He was convicted of lying under oath to the Commission that he didn't know Whittaker Chambers and had no recollection of ever transferring any documents to him.

In 1949, China was lost to the communist movement and then in February of 1950 came the arrest of Dr. Klaus Fuchs for espionage. Fuchs was one of the distinguished nuclear physicists who had worked on the Atomic bomb. Shortly after Fuchs, McCarthy came onto the scene in red, white and blue. These events, coupled with the joyous defeat of Adolf and Nazism, left the American public unconcerned about profiteering on the part of American business and their trading with the Nazis. It obfuscated any threat from rightwing Nazis in American government, and put the onus on "the communist threat" and Stalin.

The stage was set and McCarthy, an Irish-Catholic representing a German-American constituency, jumped in with both feet. McCarthy is credited with starting an epic hysteria often compared to the Puritan Salem Witch Hunts promoted by playwright Arthur Miller. McCarthy accused everyone short of the Pope of being a Communist or a "pinko," including General George Marshall.

McCarthy was more anti-Democratic Party than anti-Communist Party. He attacked any Democrats - even the staunchest of capitalists and party stalwarts.

Truman had sent Marshall to China to survey the situation there. In his report, Marshall recommended that we should seek to get a union between Mao Zedong and Chiang Kai-shek. He didn't think much of Chiang. This led McCarthy to accuse Marshall of heading up the biggest spy ring that America had ever known and led to a rightwing investigation of the entire U.S. Army and eventually McCarthy's downfall.

The Rosenbergs were convicted and then executed during this era. They were the only couple ever to be executed for espionage during a time of peace in American history.

The Eisenhower administration is usually credited with bringing down McCarthy. He was also anti-communist. He passed Executive order 10450, which intensified Truman's system of making government employment a privilege and not a right. This was a battle between Republicans and rightwing Republicans. Most mainstream Republicans didn't like McCarthy any more than the Democrats. McCarthy's tactics were underhanded and abusive and he was personally brash, rude and belligerent. Eisenhower was ready to split the party if push came to shove. Eisenhower thought Truman had handled McCarthy all wrong; "In sheer political terms I was increasingly convinced that I would defeat him by ignoring him." Eisenhower considered McCarthy a big-mouthed attention getter. His goal was to give the man as little attention and press as possible.

But when McCarthy and Cohn got into a battle with the Army over the drafting of Schine - McCarthy and company had bit off more than they could chew. When he started calling U.S. war generals Communists, the Army formed ranks and fought back. It wasn't long before the Army and Eisenhower had McCarthy backing up.

Many thought McCarthy was pushing for the presidency. His lies, fabrications, and total lack of moral ethics may really have had more to do with his downfall than the efforts of his opponents.

But were there really Democrats who were sympathetic to the Communists in the U.S. government?

There were plenty, just as there were people in the Republican Party who were sympathetic to the Nazis. There were people who were pro-Communist and people who were pro-Nazi working daily in the Roosevelt Cabinet and administration - and Roosevelt knew it. Roosevelt wanted everybody out in the open where he could keep track of them.

After the War the U.S could have gone either right or left. That is why McCarthy becomes important as an historical figure. Instead of having Congress investigating people in the government and the business community who had been carrying on treasonous activities with Hitler, McCarthy actually succeeded in turning the focus on the Communists and turning people who had supported an ally into traitors. It was a truly masterful "spinning" of circumstances and events and, of course, Uncle Joe Stalin did not do anything to hurt the cause either. Throughout the entire population of the United States there were pro-Communists and pro-Nazis. The country had been divided on which side to support right up to December 7, 1941.

McCarthy was without doubt an extreme rightwing Republican, but really he was not any more extreme than many of the rightwing Republicans of today. Many Americans supported McCarthy and McCarthyism. Many Americans supported Hitler and Nazism. And many Americans supported Marx and communism and Norman Thomas and socialism and labor and unionism. All the very same battles and arguments go on today.

McCarthy lost his Senate seat, became an alcoholic and died in 1957.

John Pierpont Morgan (1837- 1913)

"Morgan the Magnificent - if ever there thrived a money potentate whose fortune was preeminently eulogized as having been acquired by purity of method, that man was J. Pierpont Morgan." Gustavus Myers.

J.P. Morgan, unlike Rockefeller and Jay Gould, was not only adept in business and finance, but also in the art of personal propaganda.

His father, Junius S. Morgan, was a millionaire, and he was involved and became a partner with a George Peabody of the Peabody Company. George Peabody and Company was appointed the financial representatives in England of the United States of America at the onset of the Civil War. Mr. Gustavus Myers - author, historian and journalist - claims in his book *History of the Great American Fortunes*, that they were guilty of "the most active treason." He accuses them of conspiring with the British on behalf of the Confederacy against the Union Government while all the while being on the Union Government payroll.

J. Pierpont was a chip off the old block. At age twenty-four he pulled his first big deal.

In 1857 inspectors condemned a large number of Hall's carbines as dangerous and unserviceable. About five thousand of these rifles remained in the army arsenal in New York City in 1861. Via a couple of intermediaries (Arthur M. Eastman and Simon Stevens) Morgan offered to purchase these five thousand rifles for $3.50 each. On August 5, 1861, General Fremont, at St. Louis, was offered these "new carbines, in perfect condition." He agreed to buy them. The rifles were still in the New York arsenal and still owned by the U.S. government at the time of the purchase. Morgan, after getting the order from Fremont, then notified his agents in New York to purchase the defective, condemned carbines. The carbines were bought for $3.50 each and sold to Fremont for $22.00 each. This was a $92,426 profit for Morgan and friends.

In an investigation in 1862 by one of the select Congressional Committees, the following was stated in their report:

"The Government not only sold one day, for $17,486, arms which it had agreed the day before to repurchase for $109,912 - making a loss to the United States of $92,426 - but virtually furnished the money to pay itself the $17,486 which it received."

Upon investigation the Government decided that it had been cheated, but because the guns were ordered, delivered and issued to soldiers on the battlefield, they agreed to pay Morgan $13.31 per rifle. Morgan took the payment of $55,550 but then proceeded to sue the Government for breach of contract. The court, under a Judge Peck, ruled that a contract is a contract and that the government must pay Morgan the full amount agreed upon.

The soldiers who had these rifles explode in their faces due to their defective firing pins had no lawyers, never knew about their weapons being defective to start with, or were too dead to bother to sue anybody.

In the History of American Business and Industry published by American Heritage Publishing Co. and edited by American Heritage and Business Week - on page 194, I read about "The Morgan Gold Rescue." In this scenario Morgan is hailed as the banking hero who came in to rescue president Grover Cleveland who was undergoing a mysterious gold shortage in the U.S. Treasury. Morgan, patriotically, offered to buy hundreds of millions of dollars worth of Government bonds with gold from his vaults in order that the government could maintain its Treasury Reserve of gold required by law.

Mr. Myers in his book has a much different story to tell. The mysterious loss of gold in the Treasury, Mr. Myers claims, was brought on by Morgan and friends in the first place.

Morgan and his banking associates all over the nation began turning in their gold certificates and notes. Very shortly it was the banks themselves that had all of the government's gold in their various vaults. The banks did this knowing that the government would then be forced to issue bonds. This was exactly what the Treasury was forced to do. But Grover Cleveland, rather stupidly, was influenced to sell this bond issue to the Morgan banks. The Morgan banks quickly bought up all the government bonds at a low price and a high paying interest rate to them. They immediately sold the bonds at an even higher price, got themselves millions more in redeemable gold notes and quickly turned them in for more Treasury gold. Thus they had the government caught in a revolving door whereby they not only bankrupted the Treasury of its present gold reserve, but by trafficking the bonds on this money merry-go-round, they could also bankrupt future generations of Americans with a looming National Debt.

Newspapers finally got hold of the story and exposed the swindle to the people. The public outcry forced Cleveland to dump the Morgan syndicate and make a public, properly floated, bond issue which sold bonds directly to investors thus putting a stop to the revolving gold door.

Morgan and company did manage to gain themselves 62 million in bonds but America was saved the swindle on the additional 200 million dollar bond issue that the government had been forced into by Mr. Morgan and friends.

John Stossel (1947-)

"Slight of Mind"

John Stossel has developed a very interesting technique. I call it "slight of mind." Magicians perform what they call "slight of hand" where right before our very eyes they are able to make things change or even disappear. It's magic.

John Stossel does a similar trick. He takes conventional wisdom - accepted truism - and right before our common sense or rational thinking process, he is able to make it all disappear or change from a matter of importance to something that is inconsequential and more often silly and nonsensical. He turns up into down and wrong into right. And he does it right before our mind.

It is wonderful to watch him perform his act each week but, unfortunately, I have lost interest. Whenever I see John Stossel on the tube I take my magic wand and flip the channel. I do this in self-defense. Just like I push myself away from the table in order to avoid getting fat; I push myself away from John Stossel in order to avoid becoming stupid.

I have read and studied all my life in the attempt to learn to think correctly; to form proper decisions; to come to reasonable conclusions; to leave no stone unturned. John Stossel's "slight of mind" technique is an attempt to undermine my lifetime objective. I feel that his program is an attempt to make me lose my mind; my rational thinking; my quest for truth and justice; my common sense. And he does this by using the very weapons that I have developed to establish my guidelines and proper techniques.

I compare him to the Moonies who used the democratic principles of Protestant Christendom to steal the churches right from under their congregation's very principles or principals. These poor Protestants, being good Christians, welcomed the Moonies into their fold and then watched their fold and its possessions all disappear.

I don't know exactly when I began to lose faith in John Stossel, but I think it was when he tried to convince me that Mother Teresa was a manipulative, scumbag and Michael

Milliken, the junk bond criminal, was the proper moral idol for my do-gooder aspirations.

He used a kind of misguided Adam Smith self-interest principle to somehow prove that an old lady who spent her life living in garbage dumps in India trying to help the poor find food and salvation was truly an evil manipulative witch. While, on the other hand, a super-wealthy stockbroker, who escalated the value of worthless bonds and peddled them to lesser educated individuals - thus defrauding them, in millions of cases, of their entire life savings, was somehow a paragon of moral virtue.

He ended this comparative analysis with the conclusion that what the courts had decided was an evil man who consciously and premeditatedly had swindled millions of people out of millions, or maybe billions, and had been sent to prison, had actually performed an act of social kindness. And that Mother Teresa who had spent her life in garbage dumps and leper colonies trying to give people hope and lessen their pain and suffering was actually contributing to the moral squalor of the planet.

I thought John had really done a good one there. I mean, that was great. I knew, like when watching the magician, something tricky had just taken place, but for the life of me, I had to admit that I didn't see it. He had performed this feat right before my mind. I knew it was a trick but I couldn't figure out how it was done.

I have since defeated most of Mr. Stossel's deceptive demonstrations by simply investigating more thoroughly than he chooses to do and gathering more facts and applying them more logically and consistently - in other words doing more "home work" and thinking it through "intelligently."

I really don't know what Mr. Stossel is doing; it certainly isn't journalism; it definitely isn't reporting; it is the opposite of educating. It is truly magical though; I guess you would call it "stupid-fyng."

Writers and

Poets

Carl Bernstein (1944-)

Executive Order No. 9835

I've just finished reading a book entitled *Loyalties, a Son's Memoir* by Carl Bernstein, the Washington Post reporter of Watergate fame.

Carl Bernstein's dad was a lawyer. He was interested in politics. He got involved in the Roosevelt administration and served on several prominent committees. He joined the military in World War II and went over to Europe to fight against Fascism and Nazism. When he returned to his home he found more of the same waiting for him right here.

On March 21, 1947 Harry Truman passed executive order 9835. This order was to trigger the American Inquisition of the late 40's and early 50's - the McCarthy Era.

This law basically stated that anyone suspected of disloyalty could be summarily dismissed from their government job. Any individual could be called before a commission on information provided anonymously. He had no right to a lawyer, no jury, no trial. He was not allowed to confront his accusers, or to know who they were. No proof or specific evidence was required. Yet, if the board found that he was suspect, he would be fired from his job and labeled as a subversive. He might never find another job. He might have to move from his neighborhood, change his name, lie, hide and keep the knowledge of his appearance before this inquisition committee a secret for the rest of his life.

This all could happen because an individual was a member of a labor union, or an associate of a member of a labor union, or a member of a club that petitioned for the rights of blacks or minorities in America. Or you wrote something positive about the Soviet Union or you associated with someone who did. You could lose your job, your career and the potential for your whole life efforts on the false accusation of an anonymous, jealous fellow worker - someone who may have had a cousin in line for his job.

Carl Bernstein's dad was one of these people. He was bigger than an unjustly accused victim though. He was an outright champion of the victimized. As a lawyer, he took it upon himself to defend over five hundred of these people brought before Mr. McCarthy and his team of government investigators until finally like, Clarence Darrow before him, he was brought to the firing line by his political rivals and enemies. He lost his status and position. He lost his Washington career. He lost his ability to practice law. He ended up opening up a Bendix coin-operated laundromat in a black neighborhood. That is how he earned his living from that time on.

This is quite a story, in itself, but there is more.

Carl Bernstein's dad, a defender of the liberal left was confronted by the McCarthy champions of the right. Two of McCarthy's prominent knights were the infamous Roy Cohn, and Richard M. Nixon.

Richard M. Nixon became president of the United States and eventually was forced to resign from the highest government job in the land in disgrace. His entire career was ruined. Richard Nixon lived the remainder of his life fending off accusations and denying his being labeled a crook, and a criminal. Richard Nixon's sad circumstance now rivaled that of his one time victim, Alfred Bernstein. Nixon was tumbled to this disgraceful position by the dedicated efforts of the son of his victim, Carl Bernstein and his associates.

Eldredge Cleaver (1935-1998)

In the process of educating oneself, as I am attempting to do, one quickly realizes that there is a tendency to lopsidedness. In other words, a person has the tendency to read what he likes to read, thus reinforcing his own prejudices rather than getting a well rounded point of view. So in trying not to become an educated bigot, I have assigned myself to read things that I wouldn't necessarily choose. I have assigned myself to read black writers, feminists, Indians, Arabs and other minority point of view writers.

My first selection in this vein was *On Ice* by Eldredge Cleaver. Eldredge is black, and he was in prison in the sixties. I heard his name but I really didn't know who he was, or what he was about. I thought probably that he was an American version of Nelson Mandela, or a man unjustly imprisoned for stealing a loaf of bread, like Victor Hugo's Jean Valjean or some such thing.

In any case, Eldredge begins his tale of woe. He is a disgruntled black male who has been persecuted by the dominant white male "red-neck-cracker" society in Brooklyn. He decides to take revenge against the dominant belligerent white man. His weapon of choice was his penis. No, he is not going to go out into the streets and beat up white men with his penis, he has decided to punish the white man by raping white women. I don't really get the logic here but I guess it is kind of the kick-the-family-dog syndrome or philosophy. I had to stop at that point for a minute or two to see if, in any way, shape or form, I could justify this type of rationale. It was a stretch, but I said okay. So let's go out and rape white women and see what happens.

But no, Eldredge does not have the gumption to jump right into raping white women. This is a little scary for him. So he decides on an alternative. He will first go out into the BLACK neighborhood and rape BLACK women (or maybe girls - little girls - who possibly haven't studied the Martial Arts. Maybe he had better conduct some interviews here first? A person could get hurt doing this type stuff, you know.)

At this point Eldredge went into the trash heap. Nelson Mandela, he is not, and any relationship to Jean Valjean is purely coincidental.

I know that there are many black people in American prisons who do not belong there, but Eldredge Cleaver does not seem to be in this category.

Clarence Darrow
(1857-1938)

"The Story of My Life"

We don't hear or read all that much about Clarence Darrow these days. He was clearly what is termed a "liberal." Actually the American derisive version of the term "liberal" may have been coined in his honor.

Clarence once gave a speech at a prison where he lectured on his theory of the nature and origin of crime and its treatment and cure. When he was done a reporter interviewed some of the prisoners who were in attendance. They all thought that Clarence was a very kind and understanding man but even they, as criminals, couldn't bring themselves to be quite so understanding about their own criminal natures as Mr. Darrow was.

Though he was an agnostic or even possibly an atheist, he believed in destiny or fate when it came to the determination of an individual's life. He felt that a man or human being was no more capable of deterring his destiny than a planet hurdling through space could alter its direction or change its course.

If there is a God and consequently a devil, I have no doubt that at the Final Judgment, Clarence Darrow will be on hand to bring before the Almighty the case for the Devil and his right to be evil. I can hear him now: "Didn't you know, my God Almighty, when you created the Devil that he would be evil and do evil things? And since you must have known the Devil would be evil when you created him can you truly consider yourself to be "all just" in condemning him now? What kind of an omniscient, infinitely loving God are you? What kind of infinite justice are you pretending to practice here anyway?"

Clarence Darrow only defended people. He was called *The Attorney for the Damned*. He never prosecuted. And there is no doubt, if you were in need of defense, Clarence was one man that you wanted on your side.

Clarence was seventy-five when he sat down to write his autobiography and his thoughts and ideas are as clear and cogent as ever. Clarence was certainly the kind of grandfather any child would love to have. There would never be any question of his support and love for you. Not that he would agree with what you did or why you may have done it - but there is no doubt in my mind that he would be there "in your defense."

So Clarence believed that everything had a plan, was determined and that we were all subject to our own personal destiny. But he did not believe that there was a "planner." Nor did he believe that the plan was fair, honest or decent. There was a plan and it was determined but it had no direction; it occurred spontaneously, moment by moment; and it was without moral integrity. It was unjust and arbitrary. It was a plan as devised by an unthinking "mother nature" whose guiding force was science, evolution and chance. That you would end up where you would end up was assured. But your position was not designed by a responsible, thoughtful Nature; nor was it governed by fair play or moral rectitude. It would be the way that it would be and it would be that way whether you liked it or not and regardless of right or wrong.

I guess one would say that Clarence was a fatalist.

I have been reading about the exploits and adventures of Clarence Darrow for a long, long time but always from the viewpoint of another observer. This is the first time that I have read and learned about Clarence Darrow from Clarence Darrow. It was different. As someone once said, an autobiography is never objective and this autobiography supports that allegation. But it was certainly one of the more enjoyable self-defenses or personal evaluations that I have ever read. But I have always enjoyed listening to philosophers expound and generalize on themselves and their situations.

Make no mistake, Clarence is a philosopher. He is a man of very strong and definite opinions. He doesn't mince any words in defending what he believes or thinks.

He has a very good way with words. There is kindness, understanding and even poetry in his style.

In this book he goes over many of the important legal cases for which he is famous. I had previously read about all of them; I have read many of his actual defenses but I have never heard about these stories right from the horse's mouth. This man is so simple in his speech, so logical and so reassuring in

164

the correctness of his stance that it is easy to see how he was so often victorious.

He lost the Scopes case (Monkey Trial) against William Jennings Bryan. Many people even today think that he actually won that case.

He defended union agitators and even the radical IWW and Big Bill Haywood but he supported World War I despite the union and labor movement's strong opposition.

This book is a descriptive lesson in the art of growing old. It is melancholy; it is thoughtful but sad. It is an old, lovable man saying good-bye to life. The very last chapter is a poem in prose.

I have always been attracted to and admiring of Clarence Darrow. I feel much closer to the man now that I have read the story of his life, narrated in his own words. He was a sentimental, tough, well-spoken, simple, logical, compassionate and ardent supporter of the things that he believed and the people whom he loved and befriended during his life.

Ralph Waldo Emerson (1803-1882)

In some anthologies you will find Ralph listed as a poet, in others as a philosopher, in others as an essayist, or as a religious leader and educator. I don't think anybody knows where to put Ralph.

My first exposure to Ralph was as a poet. I had never read a poet before in my life. I wasn't much of a reader of anything. I was going to college because John F. Kennedy had started a new junior college idea to give boneheaded sons of blue-collar workers a chance to get some learnin', and the tuition for the first semester was one hundred and fifty bucks. A friend of mine talked me into the idea.

College suddenly made me feel very stupid, and very much a product of my lower class heritage. I was suddenly rubbing elbows with a class of people whom I never knew existed. I felt very small and in over my head. The girls were prettier than any in my neighborhood, I thought. They giggled and laughed at my white socks and loafers. Their "whites" were whiter, and their eyes were brighter, and I was the son of a man whose best job ever in life was pumping gas at a Merit station up on Broadway in my hometown of Lawrence, Massachusetts. And then I found "Uncle" Ralph.

Ralph Waldo Emerson was every poor boy's favorite uncle. He told me that I was smarter than I thought I was. He encouraged me to try, and if I failed, so what, try again. I didn't even know what he looked like but I knew that he was a "smiley-face."

He didn't have one book of poetry up on a shelf, he had shelves full. And when I read them I knew exactly what he was talking about, and I knew who he was talking to. He was talking to poor people, like me. Today I think of Ralph Waldo Emerson as a cheerleader for mankind.

His dad died when he was eight; my dad died when I was twelve. He was a New Englander like me; not only that, but from my home state of Massachusetts. He was even born in the same month as me.

I read book after book by my Uncle Ralph and it wasn't long thereafter that I was mimicking his style and writing my own poetry. I wanted to fill books just like he did. I started piling up handwritten, spiral-binder after spiral-binder. If his style was simplistic and common, I was even simpler and certainly much more common.

I don't think that I have read anything by Uncle Ralph in over thirty-five years now. Maybe it is time to re-acquaint myself. I have the feeling that if I do, Uncle Ralph will not appear "common" to me anymore. My guess is he will sound more uncommon; probably more uncommon than I ever realized.

Benjamin Franklin (1706-1790)

I've just finished reading *The Autobiography of Ben Franklin*, and I have gotten a belly laugh out of just about every chapter. The man is hilarious. I really haven't decided whether the whole book is an outright tongue-in-cheek put-on, or that old Ben is just such a practical, unemotional fellow, that his guidelines for living a virtuous life sound like a biology professor trying to explain to a slow student how to rationally distinguish his left hand from his right.

The story of his courtship with "Miss Read," his eventual wife, I'm sure, is not something that Miss Read cut out of her husband's book and hid away in a trunk of loving memorabilia in an upstairs attic, along with her first love poem and a piece of her wedding cake. She was "deserving ... pitiable and a good and faithful helpmate," says Ben. And, believe it or not, she nearly lost Ben's attentions by her inability to get her parents to cough up one hundred pounds as her dowry. In fact, she did lose Ben for a good period during the negotiations. In the interim, Ben being left "hot to trot" explains that, "In the meantime, that hard to be governed passion of youth had harried me frequently into intrigues with low women that fell in my way." He goes on to explain his thankfulness at not catching "distemper" or something worse.

His battle with being a perfect, virtuous individual he compares with a man attempting to buy a shinny ax. After a few hours and some time at the hard work of turning the wheel for the blacksmith who is trying to get the man's desired ax to shine, the customer decides that a speckled ax will do just fine. This becomes even funnier when you remember that Ben is talking about his own moral character here. When put next to the hard work of becoming moral and virtuous, Ben's decision is that he would just as soon have a speckled soul to carry to his Maker.

And this has got to be the best one of all. Ben is going into his shop on Craven Street one morning where upon he finds a "poor ... very pale and feeble" sickly woman, sweeping the walk in front of his door. He asks who hired her to sweep his walk and she replies; "Nobody; but I am poor and in distress, and I sweeps before gentle folks' doors and hopes they will give me something."

Oh, my, doesn't that nearly break your heart? So what does old compassionate Ben do? Why he offers the feeble, poor, pale, very sickly woman a shilling to sweep the whole darn street. When she comes for her shilling he presumes that a woman in her obviously poor condition couldn't have done a very good job, so he sends his servant, out to check her work. The servant reports that the poor, dying, old lady has really done an excellent job - so what does Ben conclude? Does he conclude that she deserves, possibly, a permanent, fulltime job back at the Franklin plantation or something of the like? Not quite: "I then judged that if that feeble woman could sweep such a street in three hours, a strong, active man might have done it in half the time."

Ben Franklin, the grandfather of compassionate conservatism - and possibly several illegitimate children - so, what's new?

Karl Marx (1818-1883)

If Adolf Hitler is the Father of the turmoil of this last century, Karl Marx is its Grandfather. In order to understand the history of this last century, I know that I must read more Karl Marx.

My synopsis of Marxist/social and economic evolution:

The elitism of the Greeks, Romans, and Egyptians, spawns Christianity. Christianity was the radical notion that all men, even the lowest in power and economic stature, have an equal, if not greater place in the "true" Kingdom - the Kingdom of God.

In this respect Christianity was the first to claim that all men were created equal. This Christian influence, equality in the eyes of God, and the real king of all mankind, born a peasant in a stable, led to the notion of equality in the eyes of law and government - democracy.

Democracy and the notion that all men are not only equal in the eyes of God but equal in the eyes of the law was born. From Democracy came the notion of an invisible hand directing the actions of all the people through the wise and benevolent rule of an all knowing, participating democratic ruling constituency - of, by and for the people - Democratic Socialism.

The corruption of the Democratic/Socialist state by the aristocrats, and the unbalanced intrusion of a new industrially created aristocracy, spawned the revolution of the "family man" (Bolshevist) Communism. Communism is rule without class distinction by the totality of the masses for and on behalf of the masses.

I think this is a simplistic view of the Marxist evolutionary theory. The problem with this theory is that it was too German, too belligerent and not truly inclusive of the rights of all the people. It excluded the rights of the rich, wealthy, prosperous and presently powerful and actually advocated the destruction and elimination of these people. This was not evolution, but revolution. It was without doubt, a form of social suicide, spiting the nose for sake of the face.

But this was not the Karl Marx that fascinated me. The big story within the life of Karl Marx was the story of passionate romance, and a lifelong love affair, steeped in tragedy, social ridicule, ostracism and rejection, emotional and physical pain and depravation, and personal tragedy.

Karl Marx, ironically, married one of the prettiest, fairest, most loving, loyal faithful products of the "class" of people he spent his whole life trying to destroy. And she, the lovely Jenny von Westphalen, was there with him to the very end.

She was in a room in their cheap, low-rent dwelling, dying of cancer. He was in the room next to her, dying from a lifetime of painful carbuncles and an attack of pleurisy. He rallied from his own battle with death to go to her room. There, according to his daughter, they looked at one another like two teenagers, newly enamored, until she died. Eighteen months later he died, a life without her love, was not worth further effort.

What a motion picture this would be!

John Milton (1608-1674)

My preconception of John Milton is that of a stodgy, old preacher, steeped in fire and brimstone, admonishing all from leaving the path of the straight and narrow with threats of hell and service beside the devil for eternity if his ideas were not complied with. Where I got this prejudice I don't know.

John Milton was no supporter of the status quo. John Milton was a rabble-rouser. He was whipped and expelled from his studies to become a preacher. He was a Puritan and a fighter for reform in his country's Anglican Church, educational system and government. He was active in writing and promoting pamphlets and literature in support of the overthrow of his government for over twenty years. He became a rebel in the army of Oliver Cromwell in Britain's Civil War. He was Cromwell's number one propagandist.

With the fall of Cromwell he was thrown into prison, and why he wasn't beheaded no one seems to know. It may be that he was old and blind, or respect for his learning and previous endeavors in poetry and literature held his favor. But when one considers that he had actually written material advocating the murder of Charles I, the King of England at the time who was in fact beheaded, one must wonder at his luck.

In his later life and poetry, he made a hero out of the devil, who chanted in Milton's *Paradise Lost* that it was better to reign in hell than to serve in heaven. He then went on to champion Adam's disobedience in the Garden of Eden by having Adam tell Eve that in the long run they might both be better off getting the boot from the Garden because now they would be "free" and on their own.

He was a lifelong student and read and studied himself blind. Yet he wrote his greatest works while living in his darkness. He demanded to be "milked" by his daughters at all hours of the day and night, a task that didn't make them happy or ingratiate dear, old dad to their memory. One daughter is quoted as saying that she wished and hoped that the blind, old bat would have croaked. But if he had, we would have had no *Paradise Lost* or *Paradise Regained*; no *Samson Agonistes* and much more.

He was a defender of liberty and freedom of the press. He wrote a famous piece of prose entitled *Areopagitica*, in which he praised books as being even greater than the men who wrote them - men only living for decades but books living for centuries and possibly forever.

He fell in love with a little girl who drove him nuts. She didn't agree with his rabble-rousing at all. She fancied his intellectual pursuits as foolishness, and within the first year of their marriage packed up her bags and went back home to mama. Shortly thereafter she came back begging on her knees and poor Johnny couldn't resist. My guess is that with all of her faults and difficulties she had "other things" to offer. I'll bet she couldn't cook or type either. And when she did come back, she brought the whole family back with her; all of whom sound reminiscent of *The Beverly Hillbillies*.

Poor Big Bad John, let's hope that little Mary Powell's other attributes made it all worth while.

Tom Paine (1737-1809)

Whatever happened to Tom Paine? Where are the statues and monuments to Tom Paine? Where is his tomb? Never mind his tomb, where are his bones? His bones pilfered and scattered all over the world were sold for profit by grave robbers.

Tom Paine, possibly THE most dedicated patriot of the American Revolution. Without Tom Paine, George Washington, whose bought and paid for supplies for the battle at Valley Forge had already been sold to the British in a double-cross by an unscrupulous American businessman, would have been swinging from a cherry tree. At General Washington's begging Tom scribbled off a little piece of work that inspired his class; his class being those without the shoes, without the property, and without the money. And after the revolution most of them remained without and consequently without the vote and even without their promised back pay. This particular scribbling began, *"These are the times that try men's souls..."* George, himself, admitted that without this little piece of writing it may have been all over for the good guys.

Tom Paine, a grocery store clerk, and then a corset maker with no formal education was the man who inspired the soldiers of the American Revolution. They nick-named him Common Sense, from the title of one of his other works. In *Common Sense* he challenged the authority of the Kings of the World and their smartest and brightest defenders.

Tom Paine not only wrote the inspirational material that sparked the Revolution, but gave any profits to the Revolutionary Treasury. In the end, all his new wealthy friends sold him out – including George Washington. General Washington left him in the Bastille in France to rot.

Tom Paine, the man who escaped from England by the skin of his teeth, the King's number one most wanted, the man who wrote his last great work, *The Age of Reason,* while sitting in the Bastille in revolutionary France awaiting his turn at the guillotine ... what ever happened to old Tom, and his Tom-foolery?

Robert Service (1874-1958)

Everyone should read the poetry of Robert Service. Robert became known as the poet of the Yukon which is rather humorous in itself. Not that he wasn't up there in the Yukon - he was there alright. Not as a crusty old prospector, but as a rather secure bank teller. His wonderful tales about the Yukon were more the product of hearsay and imagination. This fact alone makes me smile. Just as Rudyard Kipling was never a member of the rough and tumble infantry, "Tramp, tramp, tramping" about the muck; and Robert Louis Stevenson never saw the hole of a pirate ship, "Yo ho ho and a bottle of rum." Stevenson was for the most part a rather sickly invalid who saw most of the world from out his bedroom window.

Robert Service was a wonderful "imaginer." He was an actor who wrote his own parts and played all of his characters. What fun!

But Robert isn't just a funny clown face. Around every joke and between every witticism is the pathos and tears of human existence. Robert will make you smile and cry, often times in the same poem and sometimes in the same line. Robert's poems can and should be read over and over.

When you read his poetry I recommend that you read it aloud. First read it silently to yourself, then read it aloud, and you will see what I mean. Every poem is a dramatic event.

One of my favorite collections of Robert Service poems is his *Rhymes of a Red Cross Man*. These are lip-biting, tear-jerking poems about his stint during World War I as a Red Cross driver. Contrast this with his collection of youthful joy and naiveté, prose with poetry, in his collection, *Ballads of a Bohemian* - an instruction course in how to become a poet.

Another thing that impressed me about Robert is that he was a financial success as a poet. He made money writing poetry! He wasn't a school teacher, or a professor, or a journalist. He was a poet. He wrote poems and sold them. And he did this not in the year 1242 or 1614, but in the nineteen hundreds. He died in 1958. I have recently found out that he has written other things besides poetry. He has even written an autobiography. I would guess it to be as much fun as Mark Twain's autobiography.

The most common start into the world of Robert Service would be to delve into *The spell of the Yukon* or *Ballads of a Cheechako*. If you do, I have no fear that you will be enchanted.

Robert Service, he is my main man in the poetry department. I don't think that he can be beat. You won't need an interpreter from Harvard or Yale to explain anything that he has written.

Adam Smith (1723-1790)

Adam Smith was, first, a moral philosopher and second an economist. He was a professor and he taught philosophy. The job of a moral philosopher through the ages seems to have been to recognize chaos, disorder, and evil, and then discover, within these phenomena, order, organization and Devine Providence. Adam Smith was successful as a moral philosopher, and his books sold. He had viewed the work-a-day lives of the common man in his the *Wealth of Nations* and discovered that God was in his heaven and all was right with the world - despite any obvious realities to the contrary. If he had discovered that God was undiscoverable, heaven was a non-existent product of hopeful imagination and that the world was all wrong, he would, more than likely, not have sold so well.

Isaac Newton, before Adam, had established similar value for the Universe. Isaac had determined that the hand of God was responsible for tossing the stars and the planets into the heavens and thus perpetuating motion. He then went on to extrapolate a mathematical relationship between the stars and planets which he could demonstrate accurately and named "gravity." Isaac thus established before Adam Smith the "invisible hand" of God notion.

Adam has been stigmatized by certain concepts; one such concept being the notion of laissez-faire. Adam suggested that "morally responsible" individuals, (butcher, baker, brewer and candlestick maker – as opposed to ax-murderer, bank robber, political tyrant) pursuing their personal morally responsible self-interest, will promote the general welfare in a morally acceptable manner. Today the notion has been corrupted to the idea that immoral individuals, pursuing totally immoral self-interests, will inevitably perform a moral service for the society and the world in which they live. Even our sometimes misguided religious concoctions make more sense than this.

Religion, while advancing the notion of an all knowing, provident God, still acknowledges the necessity for a hell. This implies that all and any behavior does not result, necessarily, in virtue, even in the eyes of God - He who has created all things, and possibly even economics. God forbid.

Adam promoted the idea of morally conspired self-interest over the promotion of state sponsored or even personal and individual benevolence, because promoting benevolence, unlike promoting vice, did not seem to be governed by any reasonable restraints of conscience.

In pursuit of virtue and moral excellence personalities are often developed along the lines of Mohammed, John Calvin, Martin Luther, John Brown, Billy Graham, various Popes, Adolf Hitler, Joseph Stalin, Karl Marx, Osama bin Laden; not to mention many past and modern day politicians right here in the good, old U.S. of A.

Most of Adam Smith's observations are oversimplifications, and generalizations not wholly applicable to the complicated economics of today. But Adam may have been the first to establish fundamental principles that relate to our everyday world of monetary interaction and general commerce. For the first time in history, possibly, he established a relationship between a nation's wealth and work ... even everyday, lowly, common-man type work.

Upton Sinclair   (1878-1968)

"The Jungle"

It was only recently that I discovered this book.

Upton Sinclair was born in Baltimore, Maryland - I was born in Baltimore, Maryland. Upton Sinclair was born into poverty - my roots were in poverty. Upton Sinclair was interested in the working class people of America - my interests were with the working class people of America. This book is about the meatpacking industry in Chicago - I was trained as a butcher and worked as a meatpacker in Massachusetts and in Florida and Arkansas. My first attempt at my own business was a small butcher shop in my hometown.

The Jungle is a story about poor, Polish immigrants who came to America to participate in the American Dream - I am a descendent of Polish and Irish/English immigrants who came to this country in that very time period for those exact reasons. Upton Sinclair was a Socialist - I have been studying the American Labor movement and the rise of Socialism in this country. Upton Sinclair's main character runs off and becomes a Hobo - I feel that I ran off and lived a Hobo life for several years. Upton Sinclair was a writer who attempted to change his society and the world through the written word - I am of the same type.

I enjoyed the Jungle. It was due to the outrageous exposures in this book that "pure food laws" were passed in this country. But what is even more interesting and astonishing - as Upton himself has pointed out - this book with all of its outrageous treatment of the working man - got no laws passed for the betterment of the treatment of "human beings" - which, of course, was Mr. Sinclair's main goal.

In today's world the days of the Jungle are returning. Since the 80's jobs in the meatpacking industry have deteriorated – pays have dropped; working conditions have gotten poorer; and the immigrants have returned – many of them illegal. Even the "Robber Barons" have returned – three or four companies control the entire industry. I have the feeling that this novel by Mr. Sinclair may be on the best seller list once again. What goes around comes around. And it is all coming back as one big, ugly nightmare.

As a result of this book food was processed in a healthier manner for the protection of those who could afford to buy it. Yet nothing was done to promote the humane treatment of either the cows or the people involved in this horridly exposed industry.

This is exactly what feeds my skepticism. It does seem to me that no matter what deeds or actions have been performed for whatever cause - the eventual results are negligible. The world today has advanced somewhat technologically we will all agree; but, all in all, human civilization is about the same as it has always been.

Henry David Thoreau (1817-1862)

Henry David Thoreau didn't live very long, and didn't publish very much. He was not famous during his lifetime, and almost no one read what he had to say while he lived. He died with a library of his collected works up in the attic - hundreds of copies of the same book which he had published himself and no one bought – *Walden* or *Life in the Woods*.

He is said to be an American philosopher, yet he has written practically nothing on the nature of God, or the origins of the universe, or the nature of learning or thought. His entire output consisted of a few poems, a couple of pamphlets and a book that he wrote about spending a relatively brief and inconsequential two years living in a cabin of his own construction by the side of a small lake up in New England, Walden Pond.

His philosophy dealt with the notion of how an individual could become happy, regardless of the world about him. He said that humans should not be so concerned with achievement or their acquisition of personal possessions. If they "simplified," their personal lives would be better and the world, as a whole, would be a better place. A man is only as rich as the number of things that he can do without, said Henry.

This may very well be true, but we will never know, because it has never been the case in human history past, nor does it seem that it will ever be the case in human history future.

The only part of his writing that has impressed anybody was a little pamphlet that he wrote regarding *Civil Disobedience*. Supposedly this inspired Mahatma Gandhi to lead the entire population of Hindus in India and elsewhere into passive resistance to British domination.

Henry also spent one rather not so uncomfortable evening in a county jail for refusing to pay a poll tax. Most people think that his refusal to pay this poll tax had something to do with voting rights, and the spirit of egalitarianism. But actually Henry was a war protester. He believed that the United States government was waging an unjust war of aggression against

Mexico. This poll tax was a new tax placed on citizens to fund this war, so Henry refused to pay and was locked up for an evening until somebody put up his bail in the morning.

Actually the world never noticed Henry or his protest. It would be interesting to find out how this man and his basically antisocial lifestyle took on such an aura of greatness after his death.

Henry worked for a time at his father's pencil factory. It is claimed that he could grasp one dozen pencils every time, without fail. My guess is, knowing Henry, he was not employed at his father's factory for any extended period of time.

Mark Twain (1835-1910)

Samuel Longhorn Clemens (Mark Twain), America's greatest humorist, was not really a happy man, nor did he have a really fun-filled life.

I have read nearly all of Mark Twain's travelogues and non-fiction. I guess it all stems from my Hobo-at-heart nature.

I have recently finished reading Mark's autobiography. He wrote it from the point of view that he was already dead, and therefore could speak his mind freely without fear of a punch in the nose from old friends, neighbors and acquaintances.

One thing that really made me feel good in reading the great Mark Twain's autobiography was the discovery that even Mark Twain could be boring at times.

He was obviously a nice guy. His confessions of love and then misery after the death of his little girl, who died of an epileptic seizure one Christmas Eve, are tragic. If you don't shed a tear while reading through that segment, you have no heart and have never really loved anybody.

It was also refreshing to learn that this great man of literary, fame, wit and wisdom, could be as dumb as a board when it came to business and his personal finances. He literally went broke trying to make a buck publishing his own works. He was forced to hit the road for a number of years on a public speaking tour, just to pay off his debts. He refused to claim bankruptcy. He said that his whole public persona depended on the public's faith and trust in his honesty. Filing for bankruptcy would be the end of "Mark Twain."

But he did learn from his experiences in the publishing business and eventually published the memoirs of his friend U.S. Grant. He told Ulysses that if the job was left in anybody else's hands his widow would most likely be left penniless. He did the job, and President U.S. Grant's widow was not left penniless.

Mark Twain may have been an even greater man and human being than he was a writer. I like Mark Twain.

I'm sure there are many out there today who are unaware that the United States had a war in the Philippines in the early 1900's. In *Mark Twain's Weapons of Satire* edited by Jim Zwick the reader is introduced to another Mark Twain.

Actually the war in the Philippines was a part of the war that we call *the Spanish American War*. That is the war that Hearst and Pulitzer are so famous for promoting - do you "remember the Maine."

As a part of that war Admiral George Dewey defeated the Spanish Fleet in the Philippines. The Spanish really weren't all that challenging to defeat but that victory then led to a ground war of occupation in the Philippines.

The United States' part in this occupation, in every account that I have read thus far, is a horror story.

If one takes the time to research this war one will come upon pictures of Nazi-type mass graves and disgraceful Mai Lai type atrocities with the American army under some famous generals as the perpetrators. One was Arthur MacArthur, father of the famous Douglas MacArthur; another was a General Frederick Funston who it seems indirectly called for Mark Twain to be hanged for treason; and General Leonard Wood, a Rough Rider and Teddy "good buddy" who benefited greatly from his association with the famous war-hero president. He was appointed Governor of Cuba and then governor of the Moro Province in the southern Philippines.

Mark Twain became the head spokesperson for an anti-war group called *The Anti-Imperialist League*.

Some of the writings in this book were not published while Mark Twain was alive and there are several that were never published at all - until, of course, their inclusion in this book.

If you are a Mark Twain buff you know that Mark Twain was more than just a humorist and that he had many strong likes and dislikes.

He was not a fan of organized religion. He was not a fan of the Bible. He didn't think much of the Boer War or Winston Churchill and he was adamantly opposed to America's Imperial policies under President McKinley and Teddy Roosevelt. He was not all that keen on McKinley or Teddy either.

On the other hand, though he never has said directly what he thought about the Civil War he was very admiring of General Grant and as previously stated, published Grant's memoirs for him and made sure Mrs. Grant got the proceeds.

He wrote a funny little piece about his part in the Civil War but shortly thereafter he took Horace Greeley's advice to young draftees and - went west young man.

He clearly admired the young Filipino hero and revolutionary Emilio Aguinaldo. Of course, since we were at war with the "revolutionary" insurgents in the Philippines, to be admiring of Aguinaldo was comparable to Jane Fonda admiring Ho Chi Minh during the Vietnam conflict. Many Americans in Twain's day felt exactly that way.

Mark Twain wrote some very anti-American stuff in this book. He was not one that favored the "My County Right or Wrong" slogan. He had some extremely negative things to say about patriotism and those who use it and the American Flag to spew vindictiveness and hate and lies and positive war propaganda.

So if you have always considered Mark Twain as the all American boy, pure red, white and blue rah, rah, rah, and a true replica of what it is to be a "real" patriotic, God-fearing, American, you may have some reevaluating to do here.

Walt Whitman (1819-1892)

Walt Whitman is held in esteem among the highest ranks of American poets. His name will invariably be mentioned along side Ralph Waldo Emerson, Carl Sandburg, Robert Frost, and Edgar Allen Poe. He is hailed as the poet of American Democracy, a champion of the workingman, a lover of the American spirit of independence.

He lived through the period of the American Civil War. For three years he nursed soldiers in military hospitals in Washington, D.C. His services with the wounded have been written about and praised from every quarter. Some dying and injured have written that they saw, in him, the face of Jesus; others, the heart of Christ. Doctors working the same hospitals claimed that his services were more valuable than their own. But with all this posthumous praise his life was tragic and pathetic.

He started off a success by writing a temperance novel. He celebrated his new fame by throwing a huge beer party. From this initial positive public response he went to the abject failure of his now most famous work.

He published in 1855 a book of poetry entitled, *Leaves of Grass*. Almost nobody read this book. Somehow Ralph Waldo Emerson picked up a copy and was totally enchanted. He praised Whitman as an American prophesy fulfilled, and a living embodiment of the American spirit. But this praise was short lived. There was a problem with the book. There was a problem with Walt Whitman.

The publishers of the book were threatened with lawsuits if they continued with its printing. They stopped printing.

Walt, though praised by everyone for his services in the veterans' hospitals, was fired from his government job by a prominent official for his publication of such a pernicious book.

Walt nearly worked himself to death nursing sick and dying soldiers during the war, and after it was over, he had a physical breakdown and was laid up for six months. Later on, he suffered a stroke that left him with a limp and other problems. He wandered around the countryside with a knapsack on his back filled with copies of his unpopular book.

He tried to sell them door to door. Finally a widow by the name of Mary Davis took him in and dedicated herself to nursing him for the rest of his life. He died in poverty - a poor, pathetic and physically broken man.

And why?

The poet of the American Spirit, and champion of the common man, the encapsulation of American equality, and independence ... was a homosexual. Not only that, he actually praised his love for his fellow man in his book of poems, *Leaves of Grass*.

This man, praised to be possessive of the heart and even the face of Jesus, according to many, will never be allowed into the Kingdom he so cherished, praised, and preached the glory of to the world.

Walt Whitman was immortally condemned. His life was a hell on earth, and in his death an immortality of the same torture from a yet unforgiving world and their God is predicted. The life of Walt Whitman is a truly tragic American story.

About the Author

Richard Edward Noble was born in Baltimore, Md. at St. Agnes Hospital in 1943. He was raised in Lawrence, Massachusetts. He attended St. Rita's grammar school in Lawrence, Central Catholic High School also in Lawrence, Northern Essex Community College in Haverhill and Merrimack College in North Andover.

His mother, father and grandparents - on both sides of the family - were Lawrence textile workers.

Richard lived in Lawrence until the age of twenty-seven and then migrated to Fort Lauderdale, Florida where he met his wife Carol. Richard and Carol have been a team for over thirty-five years. They have both worked a variety of jobs. Richard has been a butcher, a dishwasher, an oysterman, a fruit picker, a restaurant manager and the owner/operator of his own ice cream parlor and sandwich shop. These experiences and many more were published in *Hobo-ing America - a workingman's tour of the USA.*

Richard is retired and pursuing a career in writing. This is his sixth book. He writes fiction, non-fiction, and poetry. He publishes a column in a local newspaper. In 2007 he received a 1st place award for humor from the Florida Press Association for this column. He has since published a selection of these columns in *The Eastpointer – Life in a Sleepy, Little Fishing Village.*

Richard has a variety of interests – philosophy, history, politics, poetry, music, biography and autobiography. *Noble Notes on Famous Folks* is a product of some of these interests.

www.ingramcontent.com/pod-product-compliance
Lightning Source LLC
LaVergne TN
LVHW011157080426

835508LV00007B/453